INFORMATION OVERLOAD

INFORMATION OVERLOAD

A System for Better Managing Everyday Data

GUUS PIJPERS

WILEY

John Wiley & Sons, Inc.

Published by John Wiley & Sons, Inc., Hoboken, New Jersey.
Published simultaneously in Canada.

For general information on our other products and services or for technical support,
please contact our Customer Care Department within the United States at (800)
762-2974, outside the United States at (317) 572-3993 or fax (317) 572-4002.

Wiley also publishes its books in a variety of electronic formats. Some content that
appears in print may not be available in electronic books. For more information
about Wiley products, visit our Web site at www.wiley.com.

Library of Congress Cataloging-in-Publication Data:
Pijpers, Guus, 1960-
    Information overload : a system for better managing everyday data /
    Guus Pijpers.
        p. cm.—(Microsoft executive leadership series)
    Includes index.
    ISBN 978-0-470-62574-3 (cloth)
    1. Knowledge management.   2. Information behavior.   I. Title.
    HD30.2.P558 2010
    153.1'2—dc22
                                                    2010004692

Printed in the United States of America

10 9 8 7 6 5 4 3 2 1

To my wife Wilhelmine, who also lives and breathes information

CONTENTS

PREFACE

This age is heralded as the information age. We live in a world more filled with information than any of our predecessors. We have to deal with huge amounts of information every day, information that affects our daily life and activities. Most people want to be "in the know." From early in the morning, when we watch the news or read the paper, until late in the evening when we talk to friends and relatives, we are exchanging information, including all that comes from our emotions. Indeed, we live and breathe information, as our five senses are continuously bombarded with stimuli to interpret. It is surprising that we human beings can still survive in today's world, where so much more attention is needed than a century ago but as a species, we continually get used to the increased amount of information and learn to live with it.

As a society, we have arrived at a point where almost all information is available to almost everyone. Information is no longer scarce; instead, it's overwhelming. And in the next five years, the amount of information available is expected to increase tenfold, mostly thanks to the Internet. However, the Internet only shows information available to the general public; it doesn't include all the information stored within organizations or in private homes that is not yet accessible to the public, not to mention the information that people have stored in their own digital memory, their brain.

The sheer amount of it makes some people nervous and tense. They experience a strong loss of concentration, a high level of stress, and feelings of guilt because they still have so much to read and digest. People start to miss important information; they select from the huge quantity available and unintentionally pick out the wrong parts. As a result, they feel overwhelmed and unable to cope with the information flow.

The feeling of being overwhelmed by an enormous amount of information is by no means a new one. In fact, too much information is a fundamental problem of the human condition. People had the same problem in the old days, as humans invented newspapers, radio, and television—among other things—to increase the flow of information. Processing that information, though, is not a technological issue but a human problem. The vastly increased information flow over the last 20 years does not present any problems to technology, but our brains have not quite found the right answer to it.

We do not know exactly how people inform themselves, how they remain well-informed over a period, and how they make sense of all the information they receive. Our memory occasionally fails us—justly so, as we discuss later in this book. Our brain has its own laws. It is mainly aimed at survival, avoiding danger and acting instinctively. From an evolutionary point of view, it's obvious: Humans are unable to adjust to the growing amount of information within a single generation. One generation is nothing compared to the age of the Earth and the development of mankind.

But it is not what information does to people that counts, but what people do with information. New stimuli, emotional situations, and deviating behavior are really good for our brain. Therefore, we should cherish these stimuli and search out unusual or different situations.

However, very few people have been highly trained in how to make effective use of information. A better understanding of the characteristics of the brain is useful in determining how to handle large amounts of information.

How often do you hear people say: "Oh, if I had only known that . . ." But obviously, we did not know, and nobody told us. Probably we do not know the right people, or we don't know how to get to the information that will make our lives much easier. And we do not necessarily search out the correct information, or look in new places for it. Numerous excuses can be given as to why people do not want to change their information behavior. Fear, anxiety, or just being an information control freak: More information is hardly ever seen as a solution.

But our information behavior plays an important part in the management of information. A computer is capable of collecting large amounts of information; only we human beings are capable of, hopefully, turning that into wisdom.

So today, you may complain about the increase in information, but complaining does not help. What does? The solution lies in seeking and finding that particular information that is important to you.

In this book you will find all kinds of tips and tricks on how to lead a more pleasant life in the information society. How can you make sure you receive the information you need? How can you organize information so that it is always accessible to you? How can you avoid the feeling of being inundated with information and having no grip on your life?

To better manage information, you will need to change certain habits and learn new ones. This is only possible if you are convinced that change is needed. We often lack the will to make changes, claiming that we have no time or are simply too lazy. Do you really wish to organize yourself better and handle information in a smarter way? Then a change between your ears is required.

Better knowledge of your brain, your information-processing factory, is a prerequisite for changing your information behavior and for driving changes in other people's information behavior. One of the most effective ways is knowing how you deal with information, as described in your information profile. Only the right knowledge, attitude, and behavior will help you truly improve your information-processing capacity. You will benefit from this for the rest of your life.

ORGANIZATION OF THE BOOK

The book is divided into two parts, which deal respectively with the principles of information, people, and the brain and with measures for using information better.

Part I: The Principles

The first part of this book discusses the peculiarities of information, people, and memory. Once we know more about the brain and acquire insight into our information behavior, we will suffer less from information stress, we will be better able to organize our time, and, will have the feeling that we are more in control.

In Chapter 1, I will present the characteristics and attributes of information. These insights will demonstrate why information deserves separate attention in our daily work and life. People have a voracious appetite for information, but only a few know why.

The reasons that people collect information, and the most salient barriers to information use are highlighted in Chapter 2. I also look at the symptoms and causes of information overload.

In Chapter 3, I discuss the main characteristics of memory. Better managing everyday data means being better able to remember and retrieve information. Knowledge of how memory works will help you achieve this.

Chapter 4 is about humans and our peculiarities regarding deployment and use of information.

Part II: In Practice

In the second part of the book, I describe specific measures that you can apply, together with the knowledge acquired from information, your memory, and human information behavior. It should be noted that the measures to fight information overload, be better informed, or help you become information literate do not act as a single tool. Each measure described in this part's chapters influences and interacts with a number of others. They are by no means exhaustive or all-encompassing. These measures are selected based on their ease of use, applicability in a business environment as well as personal life and their practical use to an individual.

Chapter 5 describes an information profile that serves as an aid to understand a person's information habits. It describes a person's aptitude, attitude, and the way he or she handles information.

Chapter 6 addresses how our senses and feelings deal with information and why movement and play are part of healthy information behavior.

Another perspective on your brain is offered in Chapter 7, where attention, remembering, and forgetting information are examined.

In Chapter 8, I describe how to select the subjects that you really wish to know about and to be an expert in. This chapter also teaches you what information to allow into your brain.

In Chapter 9, smart information workers take central stage, learning how to be more productive and apply technology in the right manner.

Chapter 10 provides all kinds of improvements for communicating information more effectively to others.

Chapter 11 has a threefold purpose. First, how do you select the right people for your information questions? Second, how do you manage information workers in this day and age? Third, how can you continue to handle information in a smart way, even long after your retirement?

Note to Readers

You can read the book from start to finish, but you don't have to. Start a new way of reading. I advise you to have a really good look at the table of contents of this book. This will help you to create classifications in your mind and will make it easier to retrieve information.

Part I is mainly concerned with theory; Part II is about practice. Start by carefully browsing through this second part. Read a few paragraphs and then decide where you would like to start. Read in this book how people handle information. Discover your own information behavior. Change if you really want to change. Should you need more tips and hints in certain areas, then consult the list of references. However, the best sources of information are the people around you. Ask them questions and keep asking.

Guus Pijpers
Riethoven, the Netherlands
August 2010

ACKNOWLEDGEMENTS

Every day, we exchange an awful lot of information. From the smile of a newborn baby to the good night said by your partner at the end of the day, information is everywhere. You need to consciously remember everything, should you ever wish to find it again. Indeed, the main purpose of our memory is to predict the future.

How people really use information has fascinated me for many years; in fact, I made it my career. Practice teaches me that we are far from effective in the ways we handle information. We teach our children all kinds of technical skills. But to be truly productive with information, our kids need different skills, capabilities, and competencies—and so do all those information workers who left school long ago.

I have also learned that the human brain is very flexible. Ages before I read the word for the first time, I knew what neuroplasticity meant, because I personally experienced it. I hope that you agree with me when I say that we have by no means discovered and utilized the full power of the human brain. Thanks to our innate curiosity, we like to know more. After all, only we human beings are able to ask ourselves clever questions as well as answer them. All these new insights into the functioning of our brain mean there are just more questions to ask. The answers will certainly lead to surprising insights. I am convinced of that.

Writing this book and searching for associated literature regularly led to an "Oh, is *that* how it is!" experience. It is also highly unlikely that this book would have been completed without the expert views of all my clients, colleagues, and friends over the years. I have been allowed to temporarily borrow their brains on a regular basis. My alma maters, Purdue University in West Lafayette, Indiana; the TiasNimbas Business School in Tilburg, the Netherlands; and the Eindhoven University of Technology in the Netherlands have all provided essential support in collecting the required documentation.

My thanks also go to Alice Saunders for her superb linguistic services. Our working relationship exemplifies the new information age: We have never met; I approached her via a qualified business contact. Her living in France doesn't hamper our doing business together, the agreement was based on a trusted relationship without any signature or legal documents, and I was able to evaluate the quality of her work soon after we started.

A word of thanks also to the editorial team at John Wiley & Sons for believing in this book.

PART I

THE PRINCIPLES

CHAPTER 1

INFORMATION ON INFORMATION

Information is ever present in our daily lives. Many of us are barraged with it. Yet it is very hard to respond to the question "What is information?" We all have a vague idea of what information constitutes.

Many words express the idea of information: Consider *data, knowledge, being, writing, sign,* and *symbol,* to name just a few. But objects such as a name, a song, a picture, or an idea also contain a shared quality called information. Some information is considered more valuable than other information, typically because a person puts a higher value on it. Old information can become valuable in a new context or when used by contemporary technologies for making novel combinations. The iPod is just one example of such a technological transformation of information.

Information is more than simple data. Data can be viewed as a series of symbols, facts, or rough observations. Individually, these mean nothing to us; only when data is experienced in the correct context are we able to process and analyze it. When data changes a person's level of knowledge, we call it information.

Data, as such, is neutral. The very same data can be important to one human being and totally unimportant to another, the reason being that the context and the information receiver are different. Knowledge is more than just information. To change information into knowledge, we add elements such as experience, importance, value, understanding, opinion, and reasoning. Knowledge is particularly, some say only, in our heads. That is why it takes such a long time to become an expert or to grow up. After all, you cannot buy experience. You must acquire it in the course of your life. The more knowledge and, with it, experience we collect, the more wisdom we get. Wisdom comes with age and is nothing less than applied knowledge.

Information, on the other hand, is what we communicate to one another. To understand information, you need to understand how communication takes place and how information is transmitted with the latest technologies, among people at large, and between individuals.

These information flows convey meaning; in the business world, these flows are the basis for decision-making by employees. Some authors argue that the majority of communication-related problems in business can be traced back to an inadequate understanding of the nature of information.

Information is the glue that holds together most of our organizations. In today's turbulent business climates, information also acts as the lubricating oil for achieving competitive advantage. But why bother about the characteristics of information or a well-established definition of information? The answer is that today, most businesses are information businesses, most employees are information workers, and profit is made by having better access to and using better information than your competitor. Therefore, employees need to better understand the ambiguity inherent in information, the complexity surrounding the deployment and usage of information, and the intricacies of information.

So what precisely is this thing called information? We are so used to dealing with information in our everyday lives that we often fail to see the complexities involved. However, to be productive with information, you have to know what information is all about.

In the rest of this chapter, I will be discussing the history of information and its main characteristics and attributes. Although the word information is used numerous times each day, a single definition has not been established. Therefore, I will take one of the most salient definitions, as it shows a clear relationship between information and the human mind.

HISTORY OF INFORMATION

Around 45,000 years ago, *Homo sapiens* lived scattered all over the world. People were hanging around the savannah, exchanging noises with other cavemen, hunting: Life was good.

Slowly, these people started to develop linguistic competence via the spoken word (often in the shape of a story), via the written word, or via drawings on a permanent medium. Cave paintings bear witness to this. These paintings represented not only stories. From the hiero-glyphics of Ancient Egypt to the Minoan clay tablets and the writings of the Maya and Aztecs, graphic depictions also served as transactions between the members of communities. We could call them the first examples of bookkeeping.

The invention of the printing press in 1455 by Johann Gutenberg created a true revolution. Around that time, hundreds of monasteries with highly qualified monks were involved in copying books by hand. Fifty years later, they were out of work. Even at that stage, a team of 20 skilled workers printed 25,000 books per year. Around 1500, that was as many as 10 million books by 40,000 different authors.

Because so much information became available, people became more skillful in dealing with information. We have seen exactly the same thing happen at the advent of the Internet. The more informa-tion is accessible and available to the general public, the more people are informed on events in their immediate environment, and the more they develop a growing desire to influence it.

Even today, information reaches us in increasingly different ways. Over the last 50 years, the printed book as a medium has met with competition from many new media, such as radio, television, CDs, DVDs, and e-books. New technologies such as cell phones and the Internet have exerted a major influence on the distribution of infor-mation, which in many cases has even become available for free. In other words, we are offered knowledge in more ways and at no cost. You could call this a democratization of information.

MEANING OF INFORMATION

How did the word *information* come into existence? The word is derived from the Middle English word *enforme*, which was derived from the Middle French *enformer*, which in turn evolved from the

Latin *informare*. In Latin it meant to give form to, to shape, to form an idea of, or even to describe. Forming an idea always occurs in the mind of a person, of a subject.

Information was used in English from as early as at least the 14th century but did not get its current spelling until the 16th century. Chaucer introduced the word *information* into the English language in one of *The Canterbury Tales*, written between 1372 and 1382. In *Gulliver's Travels* (1727), Jonathan Swift applied the word *information* in a way that had appeared as early as the mid-15th century and which sounds more familiar to us: "It was necessary to give the reader this information."

Two main perspectives on information emerge: 1) information as something mental (the content), and 2) information as something material (the medium or the representation of information). The first view is often referred to as an intangible or nonmaterial entity; the second is material and informative. Paper, clay tablets, walls, or other objects give us plenty of room to write our thoughts down. There are many storage devices, even things such as the knot in your handkerchief. Almost anything can be used to store information. All it takes to store information by means of an object is an agreement that this particular configuration represents that information. Likewise, contemporary information technologies give us numerous devices that can store representations of information.

These two concepts, information and the representation of information are often confused in everyday usage, but they are different and have different properties. For example, information can be both retained and given away, as I will show in the next section. One cannot do that with the physical surrogate without creating a second physical version. Furthermore, the medium is not the message, although it may strongly affect the message. Having a radio or a subscription to a daily newspaper or even access to an e-mail system does not guarantee that a person has read, seen, or heard the message and understood it.

CHARACTERISTICS OF INFORMATION

When talking about information, we intuitively know that it is not the same as traditional, tangible, physical resources, such as ore, lumber, machines, equipment, land, minerals, or gems. These latter resources are considered limited, which contributes to a value system for their exchange. They can be depleted and diminished. No more than one person at any given time can hold these tangible things.

Information has its own characteristics. For instance, information can be used to substitute resources or to substitute automation for human labor. Information is also diffusive: It spreads and it changes. Information has been the greatest threat to oppressive governments. Information can be communicated via a commercial, a photograph, or body language; it can be hidden in the words of a novel or newspaper. Information is human; it only exists through human perception.

This section describes the main characteristics of information based on the works of a number of leading authors.[1] *Characteristics* describe features that are related to information but are not specific to, unique to, or closely connected with it.

Access

Access is a prerequisite to the use of information. Accessibility not only refers to physical access to information but also applies to knowing what information is available. The latter is often called the intellectual accessibility of information (am I able to use it?). Knowledge about information that is available means knowing how to use what is available—for instance, knowing how to use search engines, abstracts, and indexes. It also means knowing who knows what. Evidence from recent research shows that people primarily turn to other people for information, rather than to databases, the Internet, or traditional repositories like file cabinets.[2] In buildings, you could ask people on the same floor; in your neighborhood, you ask acquaintances; at home, you look in your file cabinets and computer file systems.

The popularity of verbal sources of information can be explained largely by the fact that people regard these sources as very reliable. If the other person is perceived to be an authoritative and dependable source of information, then the degree of trust is very high. Personal sources are very information rich. They often provide additional cues to the accessed information—by conveying emotion via a smile or tone of voice, or by providing extra information that the person requesting the information had not initially sought.

Scarcity is likely to be at the heart of most efforts to obtain competitive advantage from information. In this context, *scarcity* is the value of information that is new or is not freely available to competitor organizations or other potential users.

If you are familiar with an information source, you will use it first. This source of information could be anything: a document, a person, a Web site, or a physical collection. These are not always the best sources. But as long as you get a reasonable answer, you will stick with that source. Of course, there could be a better source, provided that you know the source already or wish to invest time in searching for it.

Access to information is easier for those who belong to a social group that has privileged access to the requested information. Another advantage of membership is the trust among its members. Interpersonal information sources and other related networks are readily available.

People

Information is very human: It only exists by the grace of human perception, and its receiver determines its value. Information is extremely democratic: More information for me does not mean less information for the other person. Additionally, more information certainly does not mean better information. The correct amount is often determined by the receiver of the information, who evaluates any newly acquired information using his or her existing knowledge.

Your educational background, experience, and capabilities are the main drivers in deploying and using information. Your reading and literacy levels are likely to influence your access to information. Additionally, your ability to use technologies to access information is a strong predictor of effective information behavior. The personal skills that you have built up over time in using information also help when encountering new situations.

Your cultural background decides to a high degree whether information is experienced as useful and significant. This does not just apply to the language, but also to the ethics and customs a person supports.

There is an old saying that knowledge is power. Access to information and its near opposite, hoarding information, are both subject to political and economic powers. Power can be used to limit access to information. Limiting others' access to knowledge is in itself a source of power. Putting constraints on access to information and its distribution has always been a privilege of the owner of the information.

Feelings

One of the main reasons people look for information is its ability to reduce uncertainty about events in the real world. As early as 1948, information was already defined as the reduction of uncertainty. In this case, uncertainty is related to the amount of information available: The less information is available, the greater the uncertainty. Decreasing uncertainty requires obtaining more information, but increasing information may not always resolve uncertainty. Moreover, it is sometimes impossible to completely reduce uncertainty. Take for example the stock market, or tomorrow's weather. How much information do you need to predict whether stocks go up or down? Because stocks are part of the stock market, you might need a lot of information to make your prediction.

When you communicate information, you often have specific reasons for doing so. Perhaps you wish to incite someone into action, or show them a different perspective. However, this intention also applies to the recipient; he or she has to be willing to accept a change in his or her brain.

Trust is a precondition for using information properly. People initially seek information from other people, simply because they trust them. Those people are part of their social network and have proven to be good sources of information in the past.

You could say that information has to be true for it to be called information. But this definition means that we also need a word for false information. Worse, information can sometimes be a little true or almost true, or it can be made false on purpose. That is why the human brain is important in the interpretation of data. We are able to deal with vagueness or nearly complete data. The truth is the degree of reliability and correctness as attributed to it by the user.

Medium

The medium used to represent information plays an important role. Equally important is the presentation and formatting of the information being used, as some formats are more appropriate than others in presenting particular information.

Our sensory functions can be addressed in many different ways. We may hear information on a one-on-one basis, in a group of people, or in a public speech; we may hear it privately from someone in another location through a telephone or a two-way radio; we may hear it through a public medium such as a radio broadcast or recorded audio tape. Some media may be partly visual, like public speech. Other media are heavily dependent on visual impact, most obviously television, video, cinema, and, of course, the display screen of a computer. A particular piece of information can be transmitted by any or all of these methods, although some are more effective than others in specific circumstances.

People differ in the way they acquire and analyze information. The three main informational preferences are:

1. *Visual.* About 70 percent of all people prefer to receive information by seeing images, concepts, schemes, and so forth.
2. *Auditive.* In the preferred style for 25 percent of all people, information is conveyed through sound, music and the spoken word.
3. *Kinesthetic* or *haptic.* This is preferred by some 5 percent of all people, who learn and acquire information mainly through experience, touch, movement, experimentation, and so forth.

Once information is represented on a certain medium, it is immediately shut off from those who do not have a preference for that medium or simply cannot use that medium. People with an aptitude for listening generally find it hard to respond effectively using e-mails. They would rather talk to someone directly instead of putting their ideas and reaction into bits of information. Some people are strongly visual. They prefer pictures over text. To them, a book without pictures does not read well.

Information often forms part of technology. Without its information component, technology has little value as a resource—but that also works the other way around. Information is closely connected to the technology that carries the message. A lot of information reaches us via some medium, electronic or otherwise; even our brain is ultimately a combination of chemistry and electricity.

Time

If one rapidly needs information, time is the key factor in deciding which information source to use; this is the concept of urgency. However, a second rationale of the time factor is the implicit cost/benefit analysis. Even when people know a dependable information source—be it a person, document, or something else—they often turn to other people because they can get an answer quickly. This approach also includes interactivity; if the information is not exactly right, a short dialogue can steer the information-seeking process.

Another major advantage to the information seeker is the fact that the information source can relate to his information profile (Chapter 5). Most people have a pretty good idea what the other person wants. They have already interacted for some time, so they are familiar with the seeker's preferences and information habits. Benefits can also be realized in terms of gaining access to information that is not explicitly sought for but closely related to the information needed; the possibility of follow-up questions; and less annoyance in terms of not finding what one is looking for.

Usage

A lot of information is not used in its original form. We all cut and paste bits of information, adding our own pieces, and then distribute that information as being our own original. This practice holds some risk, in that the reliability of the information must be established over and over again. On the other hand, this is often a service provided by the sender, who combines or aggregates pieces of information to explain his message to the specific target group more clearly.

The use of your information does not result in a reduction of your possessions. Unlike, for example, oil, most information is not scarce. After all, information is not lost when it is distributed. However, information does hold a lot of value to some organizations. Information on research and development of new products and services must not be made public. That is why employees in these areas are bound by strict rules of conduct with regard to information.

Information takes context into account—the context of the user and his or her mind. Only human beings are capable of picking up on possible ambiguities in a message. However, wrapped up in their own contexts, people do not realize the importance of the context to the receiver of the information (e.g., Is the language, including the semantics, understood? Is the receiver's background properly taken into account? Are situational factors addressed?).

Context also refers to timing issues and even to the physical space in which the information is distributed. Our brains often remember the physical space sooner than the information itself, simply because our brains are geared to understanding a vast amount of contextual information.

Information is not tangible and it is the only resource that grows with use. Because information never depletes, it can be reused as often as you like, or even applied in a new way. There are plenty of examples: Music, books, data on locations—all of these share information without losing it. That is why information has several life cycles.

New technologies are sometimes responsible for these life cycles. Music throughout most of the 20th century was recorded on a record. In the late 20th century, the same songs were put on CDs. These days, the same songs are provided as mp3 files, accessible as separate files rather than a collection. A single song can be downloaded, carried with hundreds of others (related or not) on an mp3 player, or played interactively through the Internet.

Moreover, some information may be temporarily out-of-date until a new request or new insights provide a fresh look on old information. The oil crisis in 2005 meant that small oil fields regained attention, partly because prices were expected to be high for a prolonged period, but also because inefficient wells could be made profitable. Information about these wells became relevant again.

ATTRIBUTES OF INFORMATION

An attribute is defined as a characteristic or recognizable quality of an object (e.g., size, color, material, shape, or age) and is used to describe, analyze, or characterize it. Put another way, a attribute is a characteristic that describes. Attributes can be thought of as questions that are asked about the feature.

Various authors have tried to identify the attributes of information.[3] There are many categories, including such attributes as expandable, compressible, substitutable and shareable. The intangibility of information is also often emphasized. Others describe attributes such as quality, currency, accuracy, and comprehensiveness as significant. Some believe that information should be seen as something tangible, physical, and concrete, while other viewpoints emphasize the intangibility of information. Due to these different (and often conflicting) views of the information phenomenon, the attributes of information have not yet been identified uniquely. Here, the most salient attributes are described in alphabetical order.

- *Ambiguity*. Information is always potentially ambiguous. We are required to interpret it within a context to identify a specific meaning. It is precisely for these reasons that the importance of the human mind of the receiver of the message is emphasized in the definition of information.
- *Amount*. In contrast to most other resources, more information doesn't necessarily mean better information. It is even hard to assess the quantity of information that is needed for making a decision. Which has more information, a telephone directory or a large newspaper? How much information do you need when asking a question? Do you give directions to the respondent in terms of the amount of information that you expect as an answer?
- *Consumption*. Information is not lost when it is given to others. It also does not diminish when it is used. Sharing information can even lead to an increased value for both sender and receiver.
- *Dynamics*. Information has an intrinsic dynamic and unarguably influences its immediate environment. It is almost impossible to study information as something separate. In organizations, particularly, information should always be viewed in relation to its deployment and its use.
- *Format*. The format in which information is presented determines whether the recipients can do anything with it. The recipient should be experienced with the medium and the resources necessary to use that medium.

- *Inappropriability*. Information is inappropriable because an individual who has information can never lose it by transmitting it. Information can be owned, but that ownership is rarely exclusive. In other words, if I have information and I give it to you, then both you and I have use of the information. Information can, therefore, not enter into traditional economic exchange, because it becomes the possession of both buyer and seller. Information is thus said to be "leaky," because when it is transferred, it may go not only from seller to buyer but also to third parties. They may be in the vicinity and acquire the information solely through, for example, overhearing it or viewing it from afar.

- *Indeterminacy*. A person who sends information has no absolute guarantee of 1) who exactly is going to receive it and 2) how they are going to interpret it. This indeterminacy arises from the fact that information usually takes the form of a coded representation of entities in the real world, which must be interpreted.

- *Individuality*. Information comes in many different forms, and is expressed in many different ways. The same information can be represented in different media, addressing different senses of the recipient.

- *Knowledge*. Information changes our level of knowledge. That is not a once-only occurrence, but a continuous process. Keep in mind that only human beings are able to turn information into knowledge; knowledge is information that has been received as well as understood.

- *Multiplicative Quality*. Information can be used to create more information or to make better decisions, which cause actions that generate more information, and so on. This is called the self-multiplicative quality of information.

- *Redundancy*. The communication of information always has an element of redundancy (i.e., nonessential information), primarily to resolve problems of ambiguity and indeterminacy. However, this apparent redundancy may prove to have value in some situations.

- *Supply*. Information is plentiful. That is why it is often not the information that defines the value, but the time and the attention it receives from the recipient.

A DEFINITION OF INFORMATION

You would think that more than 600 years of use would tend to settle a word and result in a consensus on its meaning. This has not been the case with the term *information*. Information has become the single most important word of the 21st century. Especially in the last five decades, as the various phenomena that people call information began to be objects of empirical study, different meanings of the word have proliferated.

Most people agree that information has no meaning except when it has an impact on a human being. Therefore, my favorite definition of information is:

Any difference that makes a difference to a conscious, human mind[4]

This definition emphasizes 1) that data can come from anywhere and anything, even the internal mind of the receiver, 2) that the scope of coverage is broad, 3) that the intention of the sender is not necessary for the receiver to apply meaning to data, and 4) that a perceived difference emphasizes the personal experience of the receiving human being.

The receiver of the information appreciates the information in his or her personal context, deriving (or attempting to derive) information from the message as sent, no matter the sender's intent. For example, the beauty of a book or a piece of music is that the actual interpretation of the words, lyrics, or sound varies according to individuals, as they interpret it within their personal knowledge structure.

The latter point assumes that information does not exist independent of a conscious mind. Information is intrinsically meaningless on its own and remains so unless a human being interprets it. You can send information and try to provoke a response, but you can never be sure how others will interpret the information they receive from you. Moreover, you do not know the mood they are in when receiving the message, nor do you know precisely their interests, motivation, beliefs, attitudes, feelings, sense of relevance, and so on. Hence, it is not the meaning you put into the message as a sender that matters, but the meaning the audience puts into the message.

VALUE OF INFORMATION

The value of information cannot be determined in advance, because a human being has to actively assess the information to determine its real value. To have value, information has to be transformed by human cognitive processes into human knowledge, without which no products of tangible value can be produced or exchanged.

Valuing information is also an inherently difficult task because of the unique features of information, which distinguish it from other material resources. Examples of these features are:

- Information is not depleted by use.
- Information is noncompetitive.
- Information has no inherent value in and of itself; its value depends on context and use.
- You cannot easily exclude individuals from the benefits of using information.
- The exchange of information does not imply either loss or simple redistribution.
- Before they consume information, consumers have a hard time in determining an exact value on the utility of consumption.
- To estimate the value of information, consumers use branding, word-of-mouth, and signaling as clues.
- Information has no scarcity value.
- Information is costly to produce and cheap to reproduce.
- Information goods are often priced according to customer value, not according to actual production costs.
- Most information goods are *experience goods*: Consumers must experience it to value it.
- Production of information goods involves high fixed costs and low variable costs.
- Most of the fixed costs of producing information are sunk costs, costs that are not recoverable if production is halted.
- There are no natural limits for additional copies of information.
- If information is hoarded for the exclusive use of a limited number of people, it can actually fail to achieve its full potential value for those who hoard it. If, however, information is exchanged

and traded, the value resulting from its use increases for all parties in the transactions.

• Paradoxically, when more people receive and use information, it will experience an overall increase in value.

Information is not like food or energy, of which everybody needs a bare minimum in order to survive. Information has value only when a recipient has some need for it and has the capacity to process it. The issue is how much money someone is prepared, directly or indirectly, to pay to acquire the information; that, ultimately, is the measure of its value.

What users are seeking is information that best meets their needs. Up to a certain point, each additional piece of information increases the value of all the pieces that have already been acquired. At a certain moment, the point is reached at which there is so much information that it is no longer possible to effectively use it. This is the point of information overload.

The valuation of information will never be an easy task. Fundamental to a discussion about the value of information is the assertion that it is tied to individuals, cultures, or organizations, and thereby to an identity, role, or orientation related to those aspects. An essential characteristic of information is that it has no value except when in use. People make use of the information they receive for their own benefit, combining it with the information they already have to put it to work.

NOTES

1. Bawden, D. (2001). The shifting terminologies of information. *ASLIB Proceedings, 53*(3), 93–98.
   Case, D. O. (2002). *Looking for information: A Survey of research on information seeking, needs, and behavior.* San Diego, CA: Academic Press.
   Eaton, J. J. & Bawden, D. (1991). What kind of resource is information? *International Journal of Information Management, 11*(2), 156–165.
   Fidel, R. & Green, M. (2004). The many faces of accessibility: Engineers' perception of information sources. *Information Processing & Management, 40*(3), 563–581.

Meadow, C. T. & Yuan, W. (1997). Measuring the impact of information: Defining the concepts. *Information Processing & Management, 33*(6), 697–714.

Rice, R. E., McCreadie, M., & Chang, S-J. (2001). *Accessing and browsing information and communication: An interdisciplinary approach.* Cambridge, MA: MIT Press.

2. Cross, R. & Parker, A. (2004). *The hidden power of social networks: Understanding how work really gets done in organizations.* Boston, MA: Harvard Business Press.

3. Oppenheim, C., Stenson, J., & Wilson, R. M. S. (2001). The attributes of information as an asset. *New Library World, 102*(11/12), 458–463.

Oppenheim, C., Stenson, J., & Wilson, R. M. S. (2003). Studies on information as an asset I: Definitions. *Journal of Information Science, 29*(3), 159–166.

Oppenheim, C., Stenson, J., & Wilson, R. M. S. (2003). Studies on information as an asset II: Repertory grid. *Journal of Information Science, 29*(5), 419–432.

Oppenheim, C., Stenson, J., & Wilson, R. M. S. (2003). Studies on information as an asset III: Views of information professionals. *Journal of Information Science, 30*(2), 181–190.

Rowley, J. (1998). What is information? *Information Services & Use, 18*(4), 243–254.

Wilson, R. M. S., Stenson, J., & Oppenheim, C. (2000). Valuation of information assets. *Research Series Paper 2*, Library and Commission Research Report 33, Business School, Loughborough University, Loughborough.

4. Bateson, G. (1972). *Steps to an ecology of mind.* New York: Ballantine Books.

CHAPTER 2

A LOT OF INFORMATION

Today's business is an information business. There is little doubt that information is a valuable asset that leads to organizational success; it is the driving strategy of all businesses. Recent research indicated that the majority of employees believe that their enterprise's competitiveness is affected by problems in handling information.

However, people are drowning in information. Managers complain about the barrage of information being far greater than they can handle effectively. For every decision they make, they spend more time searching for the right information, leaving them with less time for proper analyses using the acquired information.

Companies are trying to make a profit, often using information as a competitive advantage. Employees are getting more responsibility and autonomy: Empowerment, assertiveness, entrepreneurship, and independency are keywords for their new roles. Nowadays, well-informed and motivated employees are at the core of every business.

Information workers spend on average about 30 percent of the time on searching for information (this number rises to 50–60 percent for consulting and government enterprises). This search process should not be taken too literally; information that is found needs to be analyzed, processed, evaluated, organized, and stored for later reuse. The latter tasks are often neglected in the search process. Who has not spent time to find some important piece of information that, it turns out, was already in the possession of a colleague? More than 80 percent of all information is unstructured and very hard to store in recordkeeping structures. Research has shown that only 20 percent of all information within a company is available using a search mechanism. The amount of information also makes it very hard to distinguish crucial information from noise.

Often, people complain that there is too much information, but that it is not the right kind. Technology is certainly one key aspect of the availability of huge amounts of information. However, employees were drowning in paper long before the Internet entered the office. The increased availability of information from electronic sources and the many new synchronous and asynchronous communication forms that followed have most clearly demonstrated the limitations of human information processing. Our brains are not designed to cope with so much input. We are exceptional at storing information, but there are limitations to its retrieval. Human beings also have a curious nature. They also love to share information with one another, especially if they know a lot about a certain subject.

Research has found that information overload can lead to stress, loss of job satisfaction, and a decline in physical health. People may even develop a state of helplessness and inadequacy. It is apparent that, instead of enabling a person to better do his or her job, an abundance of information threatens to diminish his or her control over the situation. Even "need-to-know" information doesn't reach the information worker anymore. Employees are starting to suffer from information fatigue. They arrive at a mental and motivational state where they are no longer willing to acquire new knowledge, due to information overload. Just as fat has replaced starvation as the number one dietary concern in the Western world, information overload has replaced information scarcity as an important new emotional, social, and political problem.

We all have anecdotal evidence of too much information in our lives. Have you seen these numbers? A daily edition of the *New York Times* contains more information than the average person was likely to come across in a lifetime in 17th-century England. A typical business manager nowadays receives 2,000 times more information than in the 1980s. The average American sees 16,000 advertisements, logos, and labels in a day. A recent report[1] found that Americans in 2008 consumed 3.6 zettabytes of data (1000^7), most of it pixels. That works out to 34GB a day per consumer.

In general, information overload can be broadly characterized in two ways. The first is when information workers are given more information than they can absorb. The second is when the information processing demand on an individual's time for performing interactions and internal calculations exceeds the supply or capacity of time available for such processing.

In the next sections, I will briefly discuss the concept of information overload. Next, I will describe the reasons for collecting information and the main barriers to effective use of information. Finally, I will take a look at the most relevant symptoms and causes of information overload before reflecting on the information mountain of the future.

CONCEPT OF INFORMATION OVERLOAD

In evolutionary terms, information overload is only about 50 years old. Thousands of years ago, before Gutenberg invented the printing press, information was far from complex. However, once the printing press made information from outside the community available, the pool of knowledge expanded. As each new technology made information easier and less costly to produce and disseminate, keeping up with the flow became more complicated for each generation.

Even so, more information was always a good thing until about 60 years ago. Around the middle of the last century, we began to produce more information than we could process. At first, we still had a rather slow process of producing, distributing, and processing information. However, things started to change fast. By the end of the 20th century, people acknowledged that they were having trouble keeping up with all the information coming at them. The personal and organizational strategies they used in the past were no longer effective.

The information overload problem was first recognized and established in the field of clinical psychology. Other terms for the problem are information anxiety, information glut, data tsunami, sensory overload, information obesity, communication overload, information fatigue syndrome, or cognitive overload.

Information overload is an oxymoron. It is like drinking too much water; one cannot receive too much information. What people mean is that they do not have the capacity at that moment to process all of the information they receive. Overload can mean being burdened with a large supply of unsolicited information, some of which may be relevant. It could also be associated with a loss of control over the situation, sometimes combined with feelings of being overwhelmed. In every case, however, there is an implication that the overabundance of information forces the individual to spend more time and energy processing it than he or she might wish to. Furthermore, information overload also deals with characteristics of information such as timing issues, information processing capacity, qualitative dimensions, and subjective experience (e.g., stress, confusion, pressure, anxiety, or low motivation).

DEFINITIONS OF INFORMATION OVERLOAD

Despite the vast quantity of research, no single accepted definition for information overload exists. Some of the most salient definitions are:

- Information overload occurs when the volume of the information supply exceeds the limited human information processing capacity.
- Information overload is a gap between the volume of information and the tools available to assimilate information into useful knowledge.
- Information overload is a condition that results from having a rapid rate of growth in the amount of information available, while days remain 24 hours long and our brains remain in roughly the same state of development as they were when cavemen communicated by scrawling messages on stone.
- Information overload occurs when the information processing requirements (information needed to complete a task) exceed the information processing capacity (the quantity of information one can integrate into the decision-making process).
- Information overload is the point where there is so much information that it is no longer possible to use it effectively.

- Information overload means having more relevant information than can be assimilated.
- Information overload is a perception on the part of the individual (or observers of that person) that the flow of information associated with work tasks is greater than can be managed effectively.
- Information overload is a human condition, impacted dramatically by new and emerging technologies.
- Information overload is a combination of three aspects: 1) too much information, 2) too low quality of information, and 3) diverse formats of information.
- Information overload is a fundamental problem of the human condition with three manifestations: 1) the frustration of being unable to access relevant information, even when we know it is out there, possibly in abundance, 2) the fear that something important has been overlooked, and 3) the inability to read, process, and meaningfully act because of too many related pieces of information.

For some scholars, information overload is concerned with the individual. Others contend that it is related to the organizations where people work. Some researchers, however, believe that information overload is caused by the limitations of computer hardware and software, and therefore the problem may be solved as specific technology becomes available. What is at least clear is that the ability to deal with information depends on the relationship between tools, people, and practices within organizations, rather than on an isolated outcome variable such as information overload.

COLLECTING MANIA

Sometimes it seems that the whole world is continuously in search of more and more information. Why this collecting frenzy? There are three reasons for this: personality, group behavior, and memory. Some people just like to collect everything. They apply the rule that you never know what you might ever need that information for. They keep newspaper clippings or bookmark Web sites for future use. They definitely never make a decision without being thoroughly informed.

Our environment also provides an important impulse for collecting. If your fellow students have a lot of music, you may feel you have to keep up with them. In many companies, collecting, organizing, and reorganizing information has become a true art. After all, you never know when you might need this information again.

The human memory capacity is a reason for our collecting frenzy. We are simply unable to remember that much, so we start all sorts of information collections. The fact that we hardly ever consult these is something we simply do not think about.

COLLECTING STRATEGIES

People use a number of different strategies in collecting information. Some people *collect everything* that could be of value some day, just to be sure that nothing is missing, should there be a demand for that specific piece of information.

Some people collect information because they have to *keep up with their colleagues*. Their co-workers are collecting information, and they cannot afford to be left behind or shown up as being less informed than others. There seems to be a belief that collecting more information will enable one to *check information* one already has. Unfortunately, the opposite happens very frequently.

It is often difficult to know precisely *what information you will need*. If someone does not understand the question correctly or the phenomenon he has to decide on, then this person collects as much information as possible. In our Western world, it is also *traditional* to use a vast amount of information. We are a rational economy, after all. Our decisions are based on good information that has been weighed carefully. However, having a lot of information does not necessarily make a decision better.

The production of large amounts of information can be used to demonstrate that *a decision must be correct* because it has been based on such a large quantity of information. If the decision subsequently proves to be incorrect, then the assembly of a vast amount of information can be used to prove to peers that one tried one's best. Information enables one to *justify one's position*.

Employees often do not know exactly what information they need. Because of this *uncertainty*, most people tend to collect any information they can find about a subject. This will prepare them well in case they have *to justify themselves*. Most people do not even have to actively seek out information. It just arrives. *Unsolicited information* far outweighs requested information. The problem of unsolicited information is aggravated by the huge improvements in IT.

Understanding and recognizing why people gather information is the first step to a solution in becoming more effective at selecting and using information.

BARRIERS TO INFORMATION USE

Many personal barriers to information use have been identified. The reasons why people do not use information are many and complex.[2] Those factors, divided over three categories, can be described as follows.

Information

Information is sometimes presented in a *format* that is not accessible, in a language of terminology that the recipient does not understand, or in packaging that hinders processing of the information. Information is often reproduced in a context that does not fit in with what the user knows. The user's *information culture* might have different characteristics, which therefore hampers the transfer of information.

Complicating the issue, information that is *attractively presented* is not always true, nor it is always what the recipient wishes to hear. Information needs to be aimed at increasing the recipient's knowledge. Sometimes *nonsense* is masked as information. People are inclined to implicitly attribute value to this. Often the medium is to blame. People also take too little time to scrutinize the message or the messenger.

There is also *too much information* on certain subjects. People might simply give up because the information takes too much time and effort to process. We also often see that information is not stored because we have to process too much information in a short time. Sometimes *people do not know* that certain information even exists. They often have no idea of the many information sources that are available to them (in the public library, for example).

People

People are often inclined to assume that others have the *same level of knowledge* or *frame of reference* as they do. People are sometimes inclined to *delegate* the search for information to subordinates. It is questionable whether those employees use the correct information sources.

People often do not know what *question* to ask in order to get the right information. The context, for example, may not be not fully known. The value of *experts* is often overrated. Calling in several experts is no guarantee of a sufficiently independent opinion. Moreover, especially because of their expertise, experts have a particular perspective from which they voice their opinion.

People do not know which information is required, which information is *already available*, or where they have to find additional information. In other words, they do not know what they do not know—and if they did know, they would not need the information. People are often *afraid to admit* that there is something they do not know. They nod and confirm that they know, even though in fact this is not true.

People can also *mentally burden* themselves with too much information. However, a person does need to be *self-confident* and skillful with technical resources for finding information and using it correctly.

Many managers do not supervise business processes any more, but receive *metainformation* on these processes, often over a great distance and over different time zones and periods. Furthermore, this information is processed several times on its way to the top of the organization.

Organization

Most organizations *administer* an awful lot. The staff often has an intrinsic preference for detailed data. By doing this, they think they are efficiently dealing with information—but often, the opposite is true.

Most organizations also have a preference for *internal information*. Information that comes from outside is often treated as if it were internal information, because it gives a sense of control.

Some organizations think that having *a lot of information* is better. A high level of detail or many facts do not make the information more correct. Also, the glut of information often makes it more difficult to see the bigger picture.

The barriers that hamper good use of information are difficult to remove. Often, people are not aware of these. Part II describes a number of practical countermeasures against these barriers to information use. Now, it is time to address the symptoms.

SYMPTOMS OF INFORMATION OVERLOAD

How do you actually know whether someone has too much information or has to take in a lot of information? Fat briefcases, high piles of papers on desks, constant meetings, unanswered e-mails: none of these are actually indicative of someone suffering information stress. The experts have as yet not quite decided on this.

Two terms are often used in connection with information overload: 1) information anxiety and 2) information fatigue syndrome (IFS). The concept of *information anxiety*, introduced by Wurman,[3] is produced by the ever-widening gap between what we understand and what we think we should understand. It is the black hole between data and knowledge—what happens when information doesn't tell us what we want or need to know. As Wurman states, we are made anxious by the fact that other people often control our access to information. We are also made anxious by other people's expectations of what we should know.

IFS is a serious problem rooted in a simple dilemma: Technologies that process, store, and deliver information are advancing rapidly, while the human brain and nervous system remain relatively unchanged. IFS is simply a reflection of human physiology not being able to cope with such vast quantities of data. IFS might not exist if you were simply exposed to information you wanted or needed. The problem is the irrelevant clutter you must sift through to get to what you need. It makes people feel irritable, frustrated, angry, vulnerable, helpless, listless, slow-witted, and even impatient.

The following symptoms were demonstrated in people who were no longer able to properly process the information on offer. They are more easily *distracted* and are not able to concentrate properly. They are less likely to make an effort for other people, resulting in *less helpful* behavior and even in *disloyal behavior* toward colleagues. There is proof that a large amount of information leads to *violent behavior* and other types of delinquency. People become frustrated and develop *all sorts of illnesses*, such as hypertension and increased pressure on vital organs. Furthermore, Japanese researchers have established that prolonged staring at monitors causes a general *deterioration of eyesight*.

Employees do not always *understand information*. The main reason is that the information as offered does not always fit into their reference frames. They are also unable to match the information with what they already know. Users often do not have the ability to *select the most relevant information* out of the large pile of information they receive.

People are often *overwhelmed* by the amount of information they have to process—which preferably has to be done yesterday. Moreover, the standard is that the more you read, the more you have to process. Looking back, many also know that a lot of information is in fact non-information. When employees are *unable to process the received information* completely or not in time, the way they perform their job may suffer. Especially because of the sheer amount of it, information causes more mistakes, inconsistencies, or *useless information*.

Many feel *guilty* when they are not better informed. A number of people are unable to sit quietly and always have to read something. People *lose control* over information. Some view the Internet as an endless library and are unable to get a grip on this. People who work with information a lot, such as lawyers, accountants, managers, and librarians, often suffer from this guilt.

People are often *unable to remember* the information they once collected. A user is not able to trace where the information can be found (physically or electronically). Sometimes, they are not capable of finding out whether the demanded information actually exists. Oddly enough, *not having access* to information may also entail feelings of information stress.

Having more information positively affects someone's self-confidence, although the correctness of the information does not increase. This may lead to *an unjust sense of security*. Information is necessary when making decisions, but over a certain limit, extra information adds virtually nothing. Furthermore, having a lot of information results in a *selection problem*: What do you choose and what do you leave out when making your decision?

Scientific research has shown that having too much information is simply bad. The symptoms mentioned in this section have been found many times. Predictably, information overload is having its biggest impact in the workplace. In the next section, a number of causes that lead to the symptoms of information overload are described.

CAUSES OF INFORMATION OVERLOAD

Based on Eppler and Mengis[4] and various other researchers,[5] the main causes of information overload can be summarized into five constructs as follows.

Personal

The person and his or her attitude, qualification, skills, and experience are important elements in determining at which point information overload may occur. Obviously, limitations in the individual's information processing capacity, personal traits, and motivation are important factors. One's personal situation (time of the day, noise, temperature, amount of sleep) can lead to information overload situations.

It may also be argued that information overload is the natural and inevitable condition of the human species. Our senses, particularly the visual sense, are able to handle a huge amount of input and to identify significant patterns within it. The modern information environment, however, presents us with information in forms our senses and prior experiences are ill equipped to process.

Information

An important cause is information itself. As we have seen in Chapter 1, information has specific characteristics that differ from any other resource, which influence the way people deal with it. For example, a certain level of uncertainty associated with information remains present, even if we have ample information available. Furthermore, its complexity or format may not match the user's needs and cognitive skills required to process that information. Most information is badly presented or incomprehensible, which often leads to a perceived over-abundance of irrelevant information.

The more information people receive, the more they want. We do know that ultimately of all information received, only five percent is used. Unfortunately you do not know in advance which five percent of the mountain of information this is going to be.

Task

The tasks and responsibilities of employees are often the cause for generating of a lot of information. Many information workers have to perform duties that are not standardized. This requires a lot of information. If employees have to perform many tasks in parallel, they will spend a lot of time changing between the various tasks. In doing so, they have to check time and time again where they left off performing a specific task. This takes time and mental effort.

Work has also moved from the floor of the factory to inside our brains. More than two-thirds of our workers are earning a living by making decisions. Also, end-users perform a greater proportion of information searching, compared to professional information intermediaries. The presumption is that users will not be as skilled as information specialists at rapidly identifying a core of valuable material and hence may feel more overloaded.

Organizational

The organizational design of a company can cause certain people to have feelings of overload. New organizational forms and communications, new ways of working together (e.g., collaborative work, virtual teams), and the globalization process all create a need for more intensive communication and coordination. As a result, more information has to be exchanged, leading to feelings of information overload.

Information Technology

The development and deployment of new information and communication technologies such as the Internet—and especially e-mail—is universally seen as a major source of information overload.[6] Technological advances have made the retrieval, production, and distribution of information much easier than in earlier periods. Because the use of new information and communication media is on the rise, technical, economic, and social filters become less effective and can easily be evaded. Moreover, the same information is now accessible everywhere and is distributed through diverse media (e.g., newspapers, television, the Internet, intranets with newsfeeds, and personal communication).

As information arrives from multiple sources, the user is required to adapt not only to the content but also to the different demands made by each individual source. The user might also have intellectual difficulty in fitting information within a cognitive usable framework. The medium through which information is communicated, and the manner in which it is delivered and presented, can also cause feelings of overload.

One of the main weaknesses of human beings is our tendency to become addicted to anything. I am talking of the constant urge for information and news. E-mail, for example, is a curse and a blessing at the same time. E-mail addiction shows all the signs of a mechanism that psychologists call "operant conditioning." Pavlov's dog did not get a reward every time the scientist rang the little bell, but, the occasional cookie—or in this case, the possibility of a new e-mail message—was sufficient motivation for continuing. As a result, we find ourselves constantly checking for new e-mail.

INFORMATION OVERLOAD TODAY

History has shown that many people in the past perceived some sort of information overload. The explosion of book production in the 15th and 16th centuries could easily be seen as information overload within that time context. Others have proposed an opposite view: Overload is an exaggerated difficulty, they say. One is overloaded only to the extent that one wishes to be overloaded. This raises the question whether perceptions of information overload are related to the quantity or to the quality of the information received.

Part of the answer to whether information overload exists is related to the information worker discussion. We are at the beginning of the information age; we simply have not yet figured out how to deal effectively with large volumes of information, or even with finding the right information somewhere out there. Individuals have space and time limitations; information doesn't.

As shown, information overload does not have one specific cause or symptom. But overload is not always a problem. It is easy to blame technology as the main cause, but are we ourselves physically and mentally equipped to be dealing with large or even specific amounts of relevant information? It can be a matter of simply installing the right resources for filtering, developing new skills, or training our executives not to demand so much information.

Physically, we are what we are. Our brains have remained structurally consistent for more than 50,000 years, but exposure to information in this new century has increased by a factor of thousands. People will continue to be exposed to extraneous, irrelevant information in the future. More and more information will be given to answer questions that have not yet been asked.

The focus should be less on the acquisition of information than on the execution of information processes: thinking about and interacting with information. There is no easy way to sift through the information mountain, but adopting some of the measures described in Part II can help us become more literate and productive with information. But first, let's turn to our digital brain and the behavioral side of information.

NOTES

1. Global Information Center. How much information? 2009 report on American consumers. http://hmi.ucsd.edu/howmuchinfo_research_report_consum.php. Retrieved January 5, 2010.
2. Kirk, J. (1999). Information in organisations: Directions for information management. *Information Research*, 4(3), http://informationr.net/ir/4-3/paper57.html.
   Macdonald, S. (2000). *Information for innovation: Managing change from an information perspective*. Oxford: Oxford University Press.
   Marchand, D. A. (Ed.) (2000). *Competing with information: A manager's guide to creating business value with information content*. London: John Wiley & Sons.
   Schement, J. R. (2002). Information. In: Schement, J. R. (Ed.), *Encyclopedia of communication and information*. New York: Macmillan.
   Wurman, R. S. (1989). *Information anxiety*. New York: Bantam Doubleday Dell Publishing Group.

3. Wurman, R. S. (1989). *Information anxiety*. New York: Bantam Doubleday Dell Publishing Group.
4. Eppler, M. & Mengis, J. (2004). The concept of information overload: A review of literature from organization science, accounting, marketing, MIS, and related disciplines. *The Information Society, 20*(5), 325–344.
5. Allen, D. & Wilson, T. D. (2003). Information overload: Context and causes. *New Review of Information Behaviour Research, 4,* 31–44.
   Lively, L. (1996). *Managing information overload*. New York: AMACOM.
   Pollar, O. (2003). *Surviving information overload: How to find, filter, and focus on what's important (A fifty-minute series book)*. Menlo Park, CA: Crisp Publications.
6. Bawden, D. (2001). The shifting terminologies of information. *ASLIB Proceedings, 53*(3), 93–98.

CHAPTER 3

BRAIN MATTERS

For centuries, humans have been trying our best to understand the working of our brains. Artists such as Leonardo da Vinci and Michelangelo made very realistic drawings of the human brain. Drawing a true map of our brain was not possible until recently, thanks to technologies such as functional magnetic resonance imaging (fMRI). Mapping the brain has enabled us to find out a lot more about the human brain.

Our brain is a complex organ. We do not know all there is to know, by far. Why, for example, is our memory so extremely good and at the same time so immensely bad? The causes of large differences between human brains in comparison with each other are also largely unknown. What we do know is that our brain is very flexible. The brain, for example, has the ability to react adequately to change in very different circumstances. This flexibility allows humans to live in all sorts of different environments, adapting to temperature, density of information, or stress levels. The brain includes a very good search engine, but we also forget an awful lot during our life.

Our brain was not just created for retaining memories over a long period of time. Over the centuries, our brains developed so that new, different matters are given extra attention. Everything that is recorded in our long-term memory has one main important quality: It surprised us. This element in particular makes human beings unique. We use our knowledge and talents for satisfying our innate curiosity to survive as a species, but also for developing our intellect.

Only humans are capable of asking themselves intelligent questions and, indeed, answering them.

To conquer information overload and use information more effectively, you need a basic knowledge of the main storage medium for that information: your brain. Just as an art historian can help you discover the details of a painting or a sculpture, this book will show you what goes on between your ears when you process information. Once you know more about this, you will be able to have more of a hold on information, and you will better understand people. This understanding means you will be able to use your brain better, and that will be to your advantage in our information-rich society. In this chapter, I describe how human memory developed and what types of memory exist. Next, a few characteristics of memory will come up for discussion.

HISTORY OF OUR BRAIN

In the history of the human species, it is possible to point out periods that were of great importance to the development of our brain. It all started four million years ago with our distant ancestors in Africa. Those relatives used asymmetrical rocks. They were capable of making use of these tools because their thumb was positioned opposite the other four fingers. Their consciousness was limited, and they were only able to understand immediate matters: things they could see immediately and did not have to remember. Their consciousness is known as *episodic consciousness*.

The next important period started two million years ago. At that time, upright man, *homo erectus*, made symmetrical stone tools. Humans had developed a concept enabling them to manufacture tools, and they were capable of passing this knowledge on to future generations. For this, they probably used sounds and imitations.

The true revolution took place around 300,000 years ago, when humans slowly started to develop the ability to speak. We also increasingly used drawings of symbols that represented various different objects. However, a symbol could also be used to indicate something other than the object. Because people were able to link ideas to words, they were able to tell stories. Around 30,000 to 12,000 years ago, the earliest cave paintings were made; for the first time, man used an external medium for recording his memories. (Graffiti goes way back in time.)

Each period of development continues to build on the knowledge and skills acquired in the previous periods. Our memory is still using the knowledge of the past. For example, we use our episodic memory for routine affairs that demand our attention at that specific moment. We experience nonverbal communication, sounds, and imitations every day—for example, in traffic. And telling stories is an art that is used on television as well as by charismatic leaders.

Our current level of intelligence has also undergone a long development. During the various different periods, increasingly more information was stored in the growing brain. Recently, we have in fact seen more information becoming available outside the brain: via the Internet, the many libraries and the many in-house information collections. The brain has increasingly become an information processing plant.

Four million years ago, we depended on each other as a group. Our social behavior, our social intelligence, is the result of this. Our technical intelligence began to develop when man started to make tools. The development of language and writing, not to mention the art of printing, resulted in our ability to process and store information. These developments contributed to our information intelligence. Of course, many more types of intelligence can be distinguished, such as creative and analytical intelligence.

BRAIN FACTS

Around 50 years ago, people began to describe the evolution of the brain using a triad. At the first and deepest level we find the reptilian brain, which in general is said to consist of the thalamus, the cerebellum, and the brain stem. The reptilian brain regulates the basal functions, such as heartbeat and breathing. This is also where highly automated and reflex behavior is realized.

The second layer, named the mammalian brain, is also known as the limbic system. This is where emotions are regulated and memories are stored. The limbic system consists of, among other things, the amygdala (involved in aggression and fear), the hippocampus (involved in the formation of the long-term memory), and the hypothalamus (which regulates blood pressure, hunger, thirst, and the sleep-wake cycle, among other things).

The third and youngest area is the neocortex—the outer layer of the cortex—which is in two halves, like a piece of foam rubber with the familiar ripple pattern covering the first two layers. The two brain halves, called hemispheres, are connected by the corpus callosum. The size of the neocortex characterizes man and distinguishes man from (other) mammals. It enables introspection and provides us with the ability to learn intelligently.

BRAIN POWER

Some facts about our brain and its capacity for storing and processing information.

- The brain includes around 100 billion brain cells (neurons).
- Each cell is able to connect to around 100,000 other cells.
- The brain is capable of making or breaking one million connections . . . per second.
- The speed at which neurons exchange information is between 3 and 300 kilometers per hour.
- The total length of all routes in the brain is as much as 12 million kilometers.
- Even before birth, the brain is already functional for the most part; a fetus produces 1 million neurons per hour.
- Biologically, the brain is not fully completed until around the 25th year of life.
- The brain weighs around 1,450 grams. On average, this is only 2 percent of your body weight.
- Victor Hugo's brain weighed 2,270 grams; Einstein's brain only 1,250 grams.
- The brain consumes 20 percent of your energy. This is roughly 20 watts.
- However, only 2 percent of all brain cells are active at the same time. There is simply not enough energy for the rest.

- Every minute, between 100,000 thousand and 1 million chemical reactions take place in your brain.
- The memory capacity varies between 10^{11} and 2.8×10^{20} bits. Other estimates arrive at 31 petabytes. That is equal to 31,000 times 1 million times 1 million.
- A person remembers around two facts per second his whole life long.
- During our life, we process about 650 million words (27,000 words per day, spoken or written; that is, half of this book).
- All 107 billion people that have ever lived (in other words, from close on 50,000 years ago) have stored 16 exabytes of information in their memory. That is 20 times all the information that could be found on the Internet in 2002.
- During his lifetime, a person processes on average 10 terabytes of data. That is equal to 10 times 1 million times 1 million.
- The maximum of information that can be consciously processed is around 60 bits. However, for unconscious processing of information, that is around 11.2 million bits per second; a difference factor of 200,000.

The brain has developed very efficiently. The transmission rate between neurons is low (e.g., compared to computers); energy is used very efficiently and therefore generates little heat. Moreover, all parts of the brain are very small: There are no great distances to be covered, and there is little loss of energy.

Information processing is also regulated. This takes place at night, using various different processors, subsystems, and flexible storage methods. This makes it very difficult for researchers to find out what is stored where in the brain. After all, they do not know the storage methodology. Furthermore, even though certain parts of the brain are specialized, there are still many possibilities left. This becomes apparent when a brain function is damaged. Very often, a different part of the brain is able to take over the lost function. The fact that our brain is flexible is also displayed by the fact that we are able to function perfectly well under very different circumstances: on the North Pole or in Mali; in a busy city or a quiet rural area; in a relaxing situation or a very stressful job.

BRAIN METAPHORS

Man has always tried to understand his brain and used metaphors for this. Two descriptions of the brain are often used: the memory as a storage space for information and the memory as an erasable disc. The last comparison especially demonstrates clearly how man over the centuries thought about recording information. Every technological innovation has brought about the introduction of a new brain metaphor. In ancient times, there were clay tablets, bark, and papyrus for recording information, and the brain was compared to those. The wax tablet, by way of metaphor, was already quite an improvement for better understanding the brain. In a wax tablet you can capture impressions and ideas, but you can also erase these.

The metaphor of the wax tablet also shows that language is also connected with the way in which we consider our brain. Watches, steam engines, telephone exchanges, radios—all sorts of appliances have, at one time or another, served as a model for explaining the functioning of our brain (or a part of it). The advent of photography resulted, for example, in the term "photographic memory." For a short time, the hologram was used for describing the functioning of our brain, but this was ultimately superseded by the computer. In the computer, we finally seem to have found a usable comparison. Access, storage capacity, working memory, operating system: everything seems explicable when comparing our memory to a computer.

Our brain has strong similarities to the computer in regard to the processing of information. Both record information; logic plays a part in both; input takes place via senses or peripherals such as keyboard and touchscreen; information is internally exchanged electronically.

However, the differences are just as interesting. The computer is controlled centrally. The brain, conversely, has a strongly distributed control system with a number of autonomous parts. The input for our brain cells is processed slowly, compared to computers (as much as 1 million times slower). Nevertheless, we are capable of recognizing very complex patterns in milliseconds, simply because we process large quantities of input in parallel.

Man has relatively little trouble dealing with multimedia applications. We can understand a busy Web site with sound because we have different processors that are simultaneously active and are capable of processing such input. A computer is unable to do this. A new operating system for the computer overwrites all previous versions. Our brain, however, contains all earlier versions of its operating system. Furthermore, some activities are still executed by those first versions of the brain: simple, quick, and reliable.

The memory capacity of our brain never runs out. That capacity is reorganized every night. The brain selects, interprets, and revises information 24/7. That is not a defect, but pure self defense. The storage facilities in computers have to be a reliable as possible. As far as our brain is concerned, that is not necessary at all. In rats, it was demonstrated that even when a random 10 percent of the brain matter is removed, it has no effect whatsoever on the memory.

People work with people, and our brain was constructed for social interactions. Computers and their applications have only just started to understand that they need to remember who is who, what someone's preferences are and everything each user has done via the computer.

Therefore, the functioning of the brain proves to be many times more complex than the functioning of a computer. Information is not just stored in one single location. Where the information is stored exactly is not important, as long as it is accessible. Compare this to search engines: We search using Google or Bing and find information. Where this search engine is running or where the data is stored is of no interest to us at all.

Therefore, the arrival of the Internet makes the following metaphor an obvious one. After all, the success of the Internet is not only due to hypertext and links but also to the fact that the Internet responds to our way of thinking. For centuries, we have been used to thinking in connections—in other words, in links and associations.

TYPES OF MEMORY

From an information processing perspective there are three main stages in the formation and retrieval of memory: the sensory memory, the short-term memory (also known as the working memory), and the long-term memory.

Sensory Memory

Each sense has its own way of remembering. Sensory memory retains its information for a very short time, on average one single (seeing) to eight (hearing) seconds. Sometimes, for example, you think you didn't understand someone correctly but before you can finish the sentence "What did you say?" the information comes in after all. You are also able to "see" something you have just physically seen in your mind's eye, even with your eyes shut.

Short–Term or Working Memory

As a classical example of the way the working memory functions, remembering a phone number is often mentioned. The fact is that the working memory can only contain a number of elements during a short time, roughly 20 seconds. One usually assumes that the memory is able to remember seven elements, with two more or less. These are not necessarily seven numbers; they may also be objects, names, or concepts. All information that is consciously processed will go to our working memory but is also quickly forgotten if the information is not repeated.

Long–Term Memory

The long-term memory can be divided into 1) the implicit memory and 2) the explicit or declarative memory.

The *implicit* memory contains memories we did not realize we had: for example, skills we have or knowledge we possess without requiring conscious memories. These are the skills we find hard to explain or describe, such as riding a bike. A major part of these skills were learned and are called the procedural memory.

The *explicit* or declarative memory consists of two subsystems: 1) the *episodic* memory and 2) the *semantic* memory. The episodic memory, also called the *autobiographical* memory, contains our conscious memories of personal events from the past. All our sensory perceptions and corresponding emotions are stored here. Memories that are stored in your autobiographical memory are limited, as the name indicates, to you.

The autobiographical memory fulfills three functions:

1. It gives us the feeling of being a stable person.
2. It plays a communicative part in our personal memories.
3. It provides us with a frame of reference for understanding ourselves and our environment.

The second function in particular is important, because through having a well-developed autobiographical memory, we are able to develop intimacy with other people, are able to maintain social relationships, and are capable of having good conversations.

Of all the things we observe in the course of the day, only a small part are stored in our autobiographical memory. These are the stimuli that are powerful and interesting enough. It turns out that the entire "movie" of an event is not stored, but only a few fragments—enough to enable us to repeat the story in sufficient detail. Therefore, vivid memories are in fact like a photo album with a lot of white on the pages. We fill those white spaces time and time again, including new interpretations.

The second subsystem of our explicit or declarative memory is the semantic memory. This memory is used for storing facts on objects and the world around us. This is often knowledge without the matching context. This knowledge differs from autobiographical memories because it seems to be isolated. Therefore, this knowledge may be everybody's.

REMEMBERING AND RECALLING

The human mind is complex. Ask anyone what "oxymoron" means and most people will have no problem in saying that they don't know. In a split second, the brain lets us say that it doesn't have an entry for that word. Obviously, the brain is an excellent search engine. But how do we know that we don't know? The jury is still out on this.

All impressions and signs that we collect in the course of the day are stored in the hippocampus (part of the limbic system). The hippocampusisinvolvedincodingandrecordingofreceivedinformation. Because the capacity of the hippocampus is limited, all data is transferred to the neocortex, the long-term memory, during the night. When we are sleeping, there is extra brain power available, because all our senses are virtually idle. At the same time, new connections are made with already-available information.

The hippocampus is also essential when reminiscing. Storing memories takes a lot of time, probably about two years. Information is picked up from the neocortex, copied and stored with a new associative context. The main advantage is that all memories are stored in different parts of the brain, like a sort of World Wide Web. It means that they have become more or less indestructible. This also has disadvantages. We cannot order the memory not to store a certain piece of information. Whether we want it to or not, our brain will always remember something. No matter how much we would like to forget certain people or wish that certain events never happened, our brain will do its own thing.

The German psychologist Hermann Ebbinghaus has established that there is a forgetting curve. We forget almost half of the information that we receive within 20 minutes. After a day, we have forgotten as much as 80 percent. The forgetting curve for meaningful information is not that steep, though.

Repetition is key to having a good memory. The more often we repeat a fact, the more links and associations are created. We remember in order not to forget. After all, forgetting means that we cannot find certain information or are unable to find it consciously in our memory. Our internal memory appears to be influenced by our external memory, such as photos and diaries. For example, try to recall all the names of the tenth graders who went to the same school as you. That is quite difficult. Try this while looking at the group photo and all of a sudden you remember a lot more.

Memories are about the past, but we evoke them in the present. For that reason, you could also describe a recollection as an amended version of our memory. The present influences the way we recall the past and, in that way, also changes the memory itself. In other words, the present determines how we view the past.

We recall events forward, not backward. We can go back in our memories to an event, but from that point onward we relive the event in the same order that we experienced it before. In our memory, we can only keep the order of our experience. A possible explanation is that our memory is not focused on the past, but on the future. We need to be able to anticipate what is in store for us, and in this, memories may be of use to us.

Researchers claim that there are two ways of recalling information: the library model and the scene of the crime. In the library model, memories are stored just like books in a bookcase, in a neat row and properly indexed. The other model is based on the idea that memories are stored like a collection of (crime) scenes. When recollecting, the detective looks at the available information, supplements, presumes something and draws a conclusion. In practice, we use both models, depending on the time that has passed between the storage and retrieval of the memory. The longer ago the event happened, the more often we use the detective model.

Forgetting

We all occasionally worry about our memory. Of course, from time to time we all forget something without having to panic over it: an appointment, keys, a birthday, or matching a name to a face.

Sometimes we do not store information on important events, or we have the wrong associations with information as received. It also happens that we do know that we know a certain fact but simply cannot get to this information, for example, because a powerful search term is missing. When we do not continue to remember information consciously, a memory becomes less accessible.

Some people argue that their memory is weak. Major events such as 9/11 demonstrate that this isn't necessarily so. Virtually everyone knows where they were, what they were doing and what their reaction was when they heard the news on the attacks to the Twin Towers. Why we remember certain events better than others has everything to do with the context of an event. Our own autobiographical memory plays a major part in its storage. Besides, we link our own stages of life to important events. We also rewrite memories of the important events in our memory.

There are two theories on forgetting. The *decay* theory states that in the course of years, the information in our memory disappears, particularly when the information is never or rarely recalled. In every-day life, we do indeed recall an incident less the longer ago it took place. This theory is based on the idea that our memory is not permanent. Therefore, information may go missing.

The second theory is known as the *interference* theory. This theory states that everything that enters via our senses is stored permanently. Because new information is continuously added, it becomes more difficult to retrieve the correct information. Information starts to look the same and overlaps or disturbs other information. Confusion about, for example, matching the right face with the right name or the mangling of proverbs is explained by this theory.

The five most frequently occurring memory problems are:

1. Being unable to recall names
2. Being unable to recall words even though these are on the tip of your tongue
3. Forgetting to do things you planned to do
4. Losing things or finding them again after going through a lot of trouble
5. Forgetting something you have recently heard or seen

In Part II of this book, you can find the solutions to these problems.

Nietzsche once said that it was never proved that we forget things. He certainly had a point. We only know that at a particular moment, we no longer manage to recall certain things. However, these matters might still be somewhere in our brain, even though we can no longer retrieve them. Forgetting represents a serious fear for anyone who is getting old. This because most people assume that our memory gets worse as we get older. However, it turns out that people who remain mentally active have up to a 50 percent lower chance of being afflicted by diseases such as Alzheimer's.

Let us first go back to early childhood. The things we experience before our fourth year appear not to be stored in our memory. The reason for this is our cerebrum. At that stage in our development, the neurons in this part of the brain are not suitable yet for creating proper memories and for making connections. The software for those memories is not good enough yet, although of course, the brain cells are already in place. After our fourth year, memories are produced in our brain. Those memories are often visual in nature, and they almost always are about events that we were involved in ourselves.

As we get older, we store more memories. Around the 25th year of our life, the brain is fully grown. It is remarkable that after the age of around 40, we keep the best memories of the period between 15 and 25 years and in particular any events that happened when we were 20. This is called the reminiscence effect. We consider the music that was popular during that period as being the best that was ever made. This also goes for other art forms such as books and films.

The fact that we have a lot of memories of the ten years surrounding 20 is because normally, a lot happens in your life around that time. Others think that this is because our personality is mainly formed around this age. During this period in which we are very susceptible, events or accidental encounters have the most impact. Old memories are also often stored in parts of the brain that are not as easily disturbed. Illnesses or memory problems can hardly damage these parts.

Déjà Vu

One of the most interesting memories is déjà vu. We have the impression that we have been in a certain situation before. There is such a strong familiarity with the situation that we think we know what is going to happen next. Yet, in a few seconds this déjà vu has gone.

An exact explanation for this phenomenon has yet to be found. Some see it as proof of reincarnation. Some psychologists explain it as a repressed fantasy that floats to the surface consciousness. Another explanation points at a difference in speed at which the left and the right half of the brain interpret a situation. The most probable explanation states that during these conscious sensations, a temporary malfunctioning in the brain occurs. After all, there are several ongoing processes for perceiving sensory information. Because the limbic system sticks a label with "familiar" on one of these data flows, this creates a déjà vu experience: a feeling of being familiar with the situation. It is interesting that we do not remember a situation a third time. In other words, there is no déjà vu of a déjà vu.

Flash Bulb Memories

Memories in which not only the message but also the environment (the context) is recorded are known as flash bulb memories. In the case of certain events, we know exactly where we were when it happened, who was present, and even how it smelled. It is not all that strange that this type of memory remains strong. We are often reminded of it because we often talk about it. Sometimes, it seems as if everyone has flash bulb memories of the same event. Oddly enough, flash bulb memories are not all that clear and we do not store all the details.

Flash bulb memories are a peculiar phenomenon. We think we know exactly where we were, what we were doing, and who else was there—just like seeing a photo, often with all sorts of unimportant details. Normal memories are never that clear. They are gradually formed and, time and again, interpreted. You probably remember where you were when you heard about the attacks on September 11, 2001. But where were you or what did you do the day before?

Why flash bulb memories are often so precise is not entirely clear yet. By now, we do know that such a memory does include all the elements of a good story. After all, we humans are born storytellers. Where did it happen? Who was there? Who told you about it happening? How did you react? A flash bulb memory often includes all these elements. Add to that that we often tell others about a recalled story like that and this explains why we remember it that well.

Emotional Memories

The amygdala regulates emotions. This part of the brain is particularly involved in shocking or traumatic events. The reason is that this type of memory came into being as a survival mechanism. Suppose that you see a dangerous snake and you learn that you have to flee. The image of that snake is stored with its context (the emotion you experience, in this case fear). Later on, should you find yourself in a similar situation or see something that looks like a snake—even if it is just a bit of black garden hose or a dark stick in the long grass—you will react in the same way: by running away. It is better to run away once too often than never to be able to run away again.

The survival principle of the flash bulb memory is also at the base of fear memories. We have a very good memory for scary or uncomfortable situations, such as, for example, humiliation. We will never forget those; they travel with us in time. From an evolutionary point of view, this has its uses. Fear involves danger. By storing a dangerous event in your memory together with the emotional state of fear, your brain will protect you when you encounter a subsequent event that is similar to your previous fear experience. This means you will be able to react adequately and the memory of fear will become stronger at the same time. In giving us fear memories, evolution had a clear goal in mind. We are certain that this situation is properly stored and quickly accessible. As opposed to normal situations, fear activates the amygdala very quickly.

Fear is a separate emotion. There is no need to be faced with a real and dangerous situation; even words can evoke feelings of fear. Many managers will assure you that a situation characterized by red figures is stamped on their memory. You could even say that the manager in question has learned to avoid a situation that causes him fear and in future will try as hard as he can to achieve positive results for his company.

We do recall emotional experiences better and for a longer time, for various reasons. First, fear as an emotion is a survival mechanism. Even a situation where the brain wrongfully raised the alarm is stored in great detail. Second, we observe events that are strongly emotionally charged with increased attention. This allows the creation of strong connections. Third, our body has learned that it has to remember emotional situations well, because by definition these include a lot of useful information. Four, all sorts of chemical processes take place in our brain, processes that ensure that the ultimate long-term memory is a powerful one.

However, there is also a disadvantage to having emotional memories. The recorded situations are biased. Through our emotions, events are remembered in a way that fits our condition at that particular moment. It is rarely a balanced and representative account of reality. We are better at remembering negative situations than we are at remembering positive ones. Bad memories provide us with more details to remember and this creates more connections in our brain.

It is also interesting that we are best able to recall memories that are strongly emotionally charged when we are in an emotional state. Some emotional events can even become traumatic and may limit someone in his performance. Emotions are often linked to specific situations. The brain is, however, capable of separating the emotion from the event. By dealing with them correctly, we are able to forget certain things.

False Memories

The semantic memory is used for storing and remembering facts on objects and the world around us. We know where the Eiffel Tower is located. When someone says "London" instead of "Paris," we correct them. The location of the tower is stored in our semantic memory.

Personal experiences by contrast, are stored in our episodic memory. Of these, we do not just store the facts but also the corresponding emotions. An argument at work, for example, is an emotional incident. You will surely recall that argument in your memory frequently, and each time it will recorded with all sorts of nuances. You add things, or leave things out, and none of this is happening all that accurately. Such a memory is not a factual one, and it is certainly impossible to check objectively. It is very strong, though.

The fact that many years on, we remember a personal event differently is because we repeatedly think about that event. Some people insist on having seen the video of Princess Diana's accident several times. There is no such video, but some people are convinced of the opposite. They supplement their memory of this tragic accident with all sort of new details when they recollect it and store it again. We often remember fragments of a conversation or just a few characteristics of a particular situation. The rest we make up in our memory using experience from similar situations. Those false memories can no longer be removed. Precisely because these have been recalled that often, they have strong connections. We are still not able to remove such powerful recollections permanently from our memory. Therefore, it is not always sensible to trust testimonies implicitly.

Using fMRI techniques, researchers have discovered that false memories are stored in a different part of the brain than real memories. They also point out that a possible application of their findings could be used for diagnosing Alzheimer's disease. This disorder means that both real as well as false memories are affected. In normal symptoms of old age, only details of memories disappear. The essence of a memory remains intact. By measuring brain activity it is in principle possible to establish Alzheimer's at an early stage.

LEFT BRAIN VERSUS RIGHT BRAIN

The left and the right half of the brain are specialized, but this does not mean that it is possible to make an absolute distinction between them. Left stands for things like logic, analysis, speech, and language: rationality. Right stands for, among other things, emotion: rhythm, intuition, sense of humor, recognition of patterns and faces, and concentration. The right half is mainly involved in the correctness of facts and events. The left half is particularly looking for explanations for occurrences. Left interprets data freely.

Until recently, we did not know that emotions also have their own specific location in the brain. We do know that emotions are largely regulated by the limbic system and that the amygdala plays a part in connecting emotions to associations and information. More recently, evidence was found for negative emotions being connected to the right half of the brain and positive emotions to the left half.

Storing information is predominantly a task of the right half of the brain; retrieving information is done by the left half. Left performs serial tasks, while right performs tasks in parallel. The right half of the brain can see many things simultaneously. That is why we recognize faces with our right hemisphere. In short, left is the text and right is the picture. Or, put even more clearly, right is the context. A few more differences: Left processes *what* is said, right *how* it is said. The left side notes the details, while the right side takes stock.

Of course this is not a fixed division. Because of illness or anomalies, parts of the brain may take over each other's tasks. In most Westerners, the left hemisphere is better developed simply because education in our society mainly focuses on that half of the brain. In Asia, where more people meditate and languages are more expressive, it is just the reverse. It is therefore not surprising that Asian visual languages address the right hemisphere the most. Languages such as

Arabic, where vowels are often left out, also demand that the listener use context for filling in the correct vowels.

During training in which people learn to use both their right and left hemispheres, it appears that we can really become more effective and therefore smarter when both halves of the brain work well together. We cannot live without the analytical ability of the left side, nor can we do without the intuition and creativity of the right side. Both hemispheres play a part in virtually everything we do. Because of the heavy emphasis on analytical ability in our educational system, students do not properly learn how to use the creative power of their brain. Information workers who are perfectly capable of making excellent analyses but who are not creative and innovative are of no use.

DREAMING

When we have just fallen asleep, our brain is still reasonably active. That is logic: One moment we are still reading a thrilling book or watching a movie on the television, the next moment we are asleep. Our sleep goes through different stages, becoming gradually deeper. The entire cycle takes, on average, 90 minutes, and generally repeats itself about four to five times per night. After stages one through four, REM sleep starts; this phase is aptly named after its most striking quality, *Rapid Eye Movement*. During this stage, we have the most dreams and our brain is very active. The longer we sleep, the more REM sleep occurs. Newborn babies have REM sleep that lasts for as long as eight hours.

An MRI scan enables you to obtain images of organs and tissue (and therefore also of the brain) using magnetic resonance. An fMRI can do a bit more, for example, registering changes to the brain while the test subject performs a task. These tasks may be aimed at observation and voluntary movements but also at higher cognitive functions, such as memory, language, and consciousness. The advantage of an fMRI is that we can get an image of the brain in an active state with relatively little discomfort for the test subject. However, it does not show us how the memory works.

During an fMRI scan, the blood oxygen level is measured. The reasoning is that an active part of the brain requires more blood than a less active part. Nevertheless, this method does have some drawbacks; for example, we can see the track of increased blood supply, but we do not know for sure whether this is connectedly precisely with that one action. In order to ascertain that, a lot more research is needed.

Research shows that dreams are essential to the processing of information in our memory. After all, during the day we have gained many impressions, and all of these need to be processed. To arrange this abundance of information, our brain processes all of it and its corresponding association anew—at least, that is what one assumes. False information and incorrect connections are not stored. Therefore, we do not dream to forget something, but to be able to remember it better later.

When we are dreaming, all sorts of strange interactions take place. Three-quarters of our dreams are about friendly, aggressive, and sexual interactions with others. When we are dreaming, the latest data is integrated with existing information and stored in the correct manner. Dreams are stories. Not such a strange thing; the brain thinks up stories all day long.

Dreams are never boring; after all, we play the leading roles in our dreams. They are often emotional because they deal with things that concern us. We also dream strange dreams. During the day, we process offered information in a logical manner, but at night we throw all caution to the wind. It seems like we do lose control briefly. All information, no matter how absurd and surreal, is processed. That is why good ideas often occur when we are asleep: All of the limitations and "yes, but . . ." excuses are forgotten. For a good reason, the saying is that we would do better to sleep on it.

REM sleep also proves to be important for properly mastering and storing procedural knowledge. Procedural knowledge is information on actions that we perform automatically and often unconsciously. This information comes in handy when we wish to learn new actions and skills—another reason for getting enough sleep.

MIRRORING

Recent research shows that people have so-called mirror neurons. These neurons cause us to copy an action performed by someone else, either consciously or not, in our mind. This goes for movements, but also for sound and even feelings. Each action that we witness is repeated by our brain. During soccer matches, there is not just a lot of kicking going on in the field. During certain movies, the audience cries almost as loudly as the hero saying goodbye to his sweetheart. Our brain repeats the observations we enjoy, or things we must copy or learn.

However, mirror neurons do a lot more. They allow us to anticipate situations, which enables us to empathize with others. They also enable us to assess the emotions and intentions of others. This capability probably explains the mind-reading phenomenon. Mirror neurons, therefore, help us communicate with each other efficiently and enable us to transfer information without too much interference. Small children learn certain actions simply because their parents have shown them how to perform these actions. Seeing is learning.

Even as adults we can learn by looking at others, from performing certain functions on the computer to acquiring the tricks of the carpentry trade. The medieval master–apprentice relationship is still a useful one. This capability also works for people who, after a brain hemorrhage, temporarily miss a functional movement and learn to do many things from scratch simply by observing others. The mirror neurons are doing their job.

CHAPTER 4

———

WE PEOPLE

People are constantly seeking and using information as part of their daily lives. Information relating to work, leisure, health, money, family, and a host of other topics is sought from a huge range of sources. Our practice of searching out and organizing information goes far back in time.

Leonardo da Vinci (1452–1519) is perhaps the most famous artist of the Renaissance. He was also a very good observer who tried to explain everything that he saw around him. Fortunately for us, he did this by taking many notes, which included his famous sketches. By the end of his life, he had collected so many notes that he realized arrangement and classification were needed. Unfortunately, he was unable to complete this task.

Giacomo Casanova (1725–1798) is known as a famous womanizer. Not many people know, however, that Casanova was a first-rate information worker. During his life, he worked as a librarian and a spy, among other things. He was renowned for being a swindler, musician, writer, and intellectual. The combination of all those functions may perhaps seem strange, but was made possible by his good extended network. Of course, he used information on people, places, and events mainly for personal gain. Casanova had a gift for worming important information out of people. On his various travels, he came into contact with many different people. At a later stage in his life, he was often asked for advice on the design of libraries, chiefly for affluent citizens. Many top managers share certain of Casanova's traits, often using them for better purposes.

Napoleon Bonaparte (1769–1821) went to great lengths to standardize the processing of information. He took the initiative to amend the French laws from what they had been up until then and to develop a civil code. One of the results was that in the areas under French rule at the time, it became the norm to drive on the right. This also meant the introduction of a register of births, deaths, and marriages and the establishment of a single system of weights and measures, such as kilogram and meter.

During his battles, Napoleon tried to gather as much information as possible. He even wrote a book on his process, and he did not make a secret of the fact that he wanted to know everything there was to know about his opponents. He tried his best to keep the information he had collected up to date, and he wanted all areas to be mapped as accurately as possible (similar to Alexander the Great, who had collected a lot of geographical information). This was necessary for the transport of troops. Napoleon insisted that his officers not publish confidential information; certainly, he did not want to hand it to the enemy. His strategy and the way he conducted a war would certainly not look out of place in our day and age.

Napoleon was not the only one who realized the importance of reliable information. Charles Darwin compiled extensive summaries of all the books that he read. Next, he indexed these summaries so that he could retrieve the information quickly. It is interesting to know that Charles Darwin understood that his memory was not fully adequate and that he needed a system for remembering everything well. He worked on his "storage system" every single day. In those days, his information behavior must have been revolutionary.

Nowadays, each person continuously seeks information up to the level at which he or she is comfortable making an informed decision. This level is also based on the risk he or she is willing to take in not having all the required information at hand. It is precisely this point that differentiates people from one another. Each person is unique in how they define information, how they perceive the importance of information, how they process information, and how they use information. Therefore, the human need to make decisions creates a demand for information and leads to our interest in understanding information.

The behavior of people in dealing with information is to a certain extent different than their behavior with other resources, partly due to the special characteristics of information (Chapter 1). In a business environment, a great deal of effort is spent on both what users should receive, or at least have access to, and in what form this information should be presented. But what do people do with the information once they have it? Presumably they examine it and apply their judgment to determine the next course of action. The many options open to them will be human-, process-, and context-specific: they may use it to update previous information, or they may store it, discard it, pass it on to someone else, combine it with other information, embed it in a report, and so on. These observable actions are collectively referred to as information behavior.[1]

Information behavior is as difficult to define as the information concept. For the purpose of this book I will highlight some information behavior theories that hopefully shed some light on this intriguing aspect of human beings. The aim of this discussion is mainly a practical one. However, I will first present you with some practical observations.

SOME OBSERVATIONS

We come across information all day long. A number of observations on everyday information behavior indicate why we should start to pay more attention to an improved use of information.

Many people grew up in a time when it was always better to have more information. At the time, access to the right information was often limited. These days, that is hardly ever the case. All information is available worldwide. Nevertheless, we still complain about not having the right information. This often happens because we do not know what information solves what problem. Having information is not the same as being informed. We have to learn to better express in advance which type of information we need for which problem or issue. You have to already know something about the answer. Because we are creatures of habit, we tend to stick with known sources of information;

we see these sources as reliable and knowledgeable. However, as we all know, it is possible to arrive at surprising insights by means of new, unknown sources of information, including people.

In the course of life, everyone develops their own style for collecting, analyzing, and distributing of information. That style incessantly changes through all sorts of ambient factors such as new resources, new people that one meets, different working environments, and changing insights. What looks like very chaotic information behavior, could be neatly arranged a week later because everything suddenly clicks into place.

People are very capable of dealing with chaos. This is apparent from their behavior when seeking information. Sometimes this search behavior is instrumental as a result of a problem or necessity. Another time, it is for arriving at new ideas; sometimes it is even for making yourself and others feel good.

Using the latest technology, you get better information, tailored to your needs. Intelligent software agents know who you are, know your information habits, and know when you should or might need certain information. Technology can really help you conquer the information mountain by providing you with faster responses informed by a more thorough understanding and less risk. Used correctly, technology helps you work smarter, not harder. However, tools are only as good as the person using them. There are abundant examples of individuals who have the latest tools but are not able to use even the basic functions.

Information does not always get to us via our eyes or our ears. Sometimes it just "feels" right, no matter what this information is called. Much information, perhaps the bulk of information, is exchanged between people. One single look, the intonation that indicates a good or an inappropriate joke, these all say an awful lot.

People's personalities play a vital part. Some people wish to have all information before making a decision. But there are also those who dare take large risks, even on the basis of very limited information. Seeking information involves a large chance factor. A lot of information is discovered by accident.

Time is an important factor when seeking information. Some people never stop; they hope to find complete information regarding their query or problem. Others stop at the first piece of information that comes vaguely close to answering their question.

INFORMATION BEHAVIOR

As with the information concept, there exist many definitions of information behavior. Simply put, *information behavior* refers to the ways individuals approach and handle information. This includes searching for it, using it, modifying it, sharing it, hoarding it, and even ignoring it. The most noteworthy definition is given by Wilson:[2]

> Information behavior is the totality of human behavior in relation to sources and channels of information, including both active and passive information seeking, and information use.

He argues that information behavior includes face-to-face communication with others, as well as the passive reception of information (as in, for example, watching television commercials) without any intention to act on it.

Information behavior is generally understood to comprise two key activities: *information-seeking* behavior and *information-use* behavior.[3] Information-seeking behavior is defined as the purposive seeking of information as a result of a need to satisfy some goal. In the course of seeking, the individual may interact with manual information systems (such as a newspaper or a library) or with IT-based systems (such as the World Wide Web). A subset of information-seeking behavior is information-searching behavior, which is the "micro-level" of behavior employed by the searcher in interacting with information systems of all kinds. It consists of all interactions with the system, whether at the level of human computer interaction (e.g., using the mouse and clicking on links) or at the intellectual level (e.g., adopting a Boolean search strategy), which will also involve mental acts, such as judging the relevance of data or information retrieved.

The second component of information behavior is *information-use* behavior, which consists of the physical and mental acts involved in incorporating the information found in the person's existing knowledge base. It may include physical acts, such as marking sections in a text to note their importance or significance, as well as mental acts that involve comparing new information with existing knowledge.

INFORMATION BEHAVIOR THEORIES

The focus of this book is on making the reader aware of the information concept, the theories behind it, and a number of practical solutions for becoming more effective at using information. In that respect, information behavior is so broad a subject that certain selections were made from a range of very diverse theories. The main rationale behind the selection of various information behavior theories is their practical applicability in the business and private environment of the individual.

Berrypicking

Bates[4] developed her *berrypicking* theory to indicate that the search process is itself an important part of the result. With each intermediary result, the question that has to be answered is further refined. In other words, the results and someone's ideas on this lead to the desired result.

Everyone seeking information on the Internet knows the principle of "each time a little bit more." People search, find something, amend their strategy or question a little, search again, come across obstacles and so on. This process is exactly the thought behind the theory of berrypicking.

Because we often do not know exactly what we are looking for, it makes a difference which search engine or library we use. We start by phrasing the question vaguely, get all sorts of hits and search through them. We check the literature list in a book, to see what sources the author in question has used. Footnotes and references may also help us on our way. This type of information allows us to ask our questions more precisely and search increasingly further.

Closely related to this theory is the so-called *low-hanging fruit* principle. When researching something on the Internet using a search engine, we rarely look further than the first page of search results. This behavior has to do with our laziness, but it is also a factor of available time and the fact that we always find something of interest on that first page.

Everyday Life Information Seeking

To most people, work is only part of their life. An important part of everyone's information behavior takes place elsewhere. Savolainen[5] defines everyday life information seeking as:

> . . . the acquisition of various informational (both cognitive and expressive) elements which people employ to orient themselves in daily life and solve problems not directly associated with the performance of occupational tasks.

The theory focuses on small groups, and, within that, particularly on individuals and the social relationships between them. For the members of a particular group of people, access to and use of various sources of information is mainly subject to what others know about and think of these. Studies of everyday information behavior are often carried out in fields such as health, leisure, and consumer behavior.

A practical example is searching for information in case of a health problem. Suppose that you suffer from a chronic illness, such as diabetes. That illness controls your entire daily routine. Patients like to keep informed of the latest developments and ways for dealing with this illness, both at home and at work. Especially with a chronic illness, nothing is trivial. Having the right information may enable the individual to gain more control over the illness and lead a better quality of life.

People looking for information on their illness can be divided into two groups. One group wishes to know absolutely everything about the disease they were diagnosed as having. Sometimes they join patients' associations to make sure that do not miss a single bit of information. Positive news will stop these people from worrying. The other group wishes to know as little as possible and primarily focuses on getting better. One or two members of this might check out exactly what was wrong, but only after their recovery.

Incidentally, this difference in behavior often occurs in work situations. Some managers want to know everything exactly and in advance, including scenarios of all the things that might go wrong. Other managers do not want to hear anything about the way things proceed until it is all over; then, if necessary, they might have a look at the process.

Information Foraging

In the early 1990s, researchers at the Palo Alto Research Center developed the theory of *information foraging*. This theory uses the analogy of wild animals gathering food to analyze how humans collect information.[6]

Animals use all sorts of techniques for distributing information, including the use of scent. In many animal species, the nose is an extremely well-developed organ. Using scent trails, animals communicate to each other where energy-rich food can be found. This way, they assist one another in finding a healthy and nourishing meal with minimal effort. Ants, for example, leave a scent trail on an object they are crossing. That practice is not only useful to the colony; the ants themselves also benefit, as their brains do not have to perform complex calculations or searches for retrieving information each time, but simply follow the trail without too much effort.

People also set information trails, often without being aware of this. They comment on a product on a comparison site, discuss a book, or share their experience with products and services in their personal network. Blogs could be called the ultimate form of information trails.

Some organizations have noticed that it is possible to deliberately set information scent trails. Leaking information prematurely, sending a concept first or a well-known "pilot balloon"—all of these are ways to steer information behavior in the desired direction.

As far as information trails are concerned, there are a few important points of interest. The information needs to be presented attractively. A dull Web site without any pictures, a brochure that does not invite people to read it, a poor speaker—any of these can nullify good information. Moreover, the information needs to be easy to find. If it takes too much time, money, or effort to find something, people will simply skip these sources of information. Finally, it is important that information be easily accessible. If people have to go through several screens, three different doors, or several people, they usually give up.

Information Grounds

It has been said before; people prefer talking to people over talking to a system. Someone once said: "Talking to someone for just five minutes is often more informative than searching online for five hours. The most powerful search engine is man." It is part of human nature to share information. Social interactions are important to us. By talking to each other, exchanging gossip, and telling the latest news items, we acquire a lot of information in a spontaneous, natural way. It also meets our need for telling stories. People always seek out each other, even in their leisure time.

On this subject, Fisher[7] developed the *information ground* theory. An information ground is an environment temporarily created when people come together for a single purpose, but from whose behavior emerges a social atmosphere that fosters the spontaneous and serendipitous sharing of information. In places like restaurants, canteens, sports clubs, and churches, as well as in hospitals, waiting rooms, beauty parlors, and public transportation, people are not primarily gathering to exchange information, but it often happens nevertheless.

The physical contact and the immediate possibility for interaction make these places into good information sources for many people. When we are among like-minded people, we are able to receive and supply all kinds of different information very quickly. After all, our memory is trained to form an opinion on others quickly and instinctively. This relaxed way of exchanging information is very close to what people prefer. We are among equals; there's a good atmosphere; people are honest, friendly, and reliable; and most of them share roughly the same experience, background, and outlook on life. There is a vast chance of getting information that will really help you.

An information ground is also interesting for another reason. Many people have a to-do list in mind, containing all the information they still have to discover. Surrounded by so many smart people, it is easy to ask your question as if by coincidence. You will almost always get an answer or reference. This also explains why the current trend of changing to flexible places of work is so much more advantageous for knowledge management within organizations. Well-equipped coffee corners and lounge areas pay for themselves in no time at all.

Information Orientation

Based on practical experience, Marchand, Kettinger, and Rollins[8] developed the *information orientation* model. They researched the deployment and use of information by managers in large companies. Their research unit was the organization itself, as opposed to virtually all other theories, which put the individual first. Of course, information behavior is linked to a person, but Marchand, Kettinger, and Rollins aggregate this at organizational level.

The model consists of three information capabilities:

1. *Information behavior and values*—the capability of a company to instill and promote behaviors and values in its people for the effective use of information
2. *Information management practices*—the capability of a company to manage information effectively over its life cycle
3. *Information technology practices*—the capability of a company to deploy appropriate IT applications and infrastructure in support of operational, decision-making, and communication processes

Most interesting in this theory is the fact its creators explicitly give attention to good information behavior. After all, an analysis is interesting enough in and of itself, but it does not ensure that an organization and its workers indeed deploy and use information effectively. To this purpose, Marchand, Kettinger, and Rollins introduce, with each of the three parts, a maturity scale with six levels, in which each level builds on the previously acquired appreciation. Information behavior and value, for example, starts with *integrity* (the absence of manipulating information for personal gain) and goes up to the highest achievable level of *proactiveness* (when employees actively seek out and respond to changes in their competitive environment and think about how to use this information to enhance existing and create new products and services).

Information Horizon

Sonnenwald[9] provides a refreshing view on the information behavior of individuals. In her *information horizon* theory, she raises the matter of the importance of the social network and context regarding someone's information behavior. The aspects of this theory are about 1) when and why people use others and other sources of information (or exactly the opposite), 2) the relationships between the various different sources of information, 3) the active use of information sources, and 4) the influence of context during the information search process. In that case, the information horizon consists of all information sources used by someone when seeking information. Examples of information sources are the social network, including colleagues, information specialists, and experts; documents, including all sorts of media and the Web; IT resources, like query tools and information systems; and finally, people's own experiences and observations.

Information horizons differ by individual and situation. Sometimes an information horizon is limited through social or political factors. It is, for example, clear that in certain countries not everyone is able to simply access information everywhere. Persons need to know what sources are available. In this, colleagues are often helpful.

A person's information horizon often includes several information sources that can deliver the required information. It is important to find the best answer and therefore, the best source. In such a research, one typically uses a graphic representation of all information sources. One can also easily add preferences for a certain source. It may be clear that a picture with weighed sources of information and the links between these forms a powerful tool for starting a discussion. A picture is very intuitive, and it helps people focus their attention. Any gaps or missing links can be traced quickly. When combined with techniques such as *mind-mapping*, the result can also be shared easily within a team.

Keeping Found Things Found

Many people occasionally complain they cannot find a certain item. They know they put it somewhere, they just cannot remember where. The shoebox full of photos has not disappeared; it still exists, next to extra collections such as the files with digital photos on our personal computer. Only a few people organize their collections like a librarian. They think that organizing will take too much time and will bring only small advantages. They prefer to rely on their memory for finding what they once stored. However, they forget that their memory is many times worse at organizing information collections than an automated system.

It is estimated that knowledge workers spend 15–35 percent of their time in an attempt to find information, again. Almost half of all workers are unable to find information, even within their own company. A lot of information is already in our possession but we have forgotten we have it. This means that we will not go looking for it. Many searches are canceled, sometimes with restrained anger, because you are sure that this information has to be somewhere. These days, even well-organized colleagues are often unable to find things again, simply because they have so many things. That is why someone once sighed: "If only we knew what we know already."

Jones[10] developed the *keeping found things found* theory, which emphasizes that we find a lot of information but soon lose it. This does not apply to our memory alone, but also to physical things. Even worse, we know that we put it somewhere, but we are unable to find it again. He stresses the importance of well-organized personal information collections. These are not necessarily physical collections. Digital information collections also need maintenance. The fact that the collections are individual ones only makes the problems worse. We rarely know the criteria on which another person selects, arranges, and saves.

Retrieving information, in no matter what form, involves several important factors. First, the time you have available is important. Sometimes it is indeed easier to create new information than to put time and effort into a fruitless search. Second, another person's help may often be a real boon—not because he or she knows where you stored this information, but because he or she will ask questions such as: "What were you doing when you got the information?" or "Where were you when you stored it?" Sometimes they know better than you how to use the specific search engine on your computer. Third, you will retrieve information more quickly when you become more selective and throw more out. After all, when the information mountain is not too high, it is easier to find the information you need. Fourth, your own personality is an important factor in your search for information. Some people really keep absolutely everything, and for a very long time. Others have no trouble at all and cut back their information collections on a regular basis. Finally, a lot of information is linked to specific persons. We often remember who gave us the information better than the place we stored it. These days, there are search techniques that take this factor into account.

Principle of Least Effort

Most people are very, very busy—at least, that is what they say. Somehow, these people realize that they are a little lazy. Why do it yourself, if others can do it better?

We would rather choose the easiest path when we need information. After all, asking someone to explain something is easier than reading the entire manual yourself. In this way, quality and reliability often lose out on convenience, time, and cost savings. We often prefer to stick with known sources of information, because they are familiar. The well-known trial and error when seeking information also often produces good (that is, sufficient) information. Besides, it takes less energy. People are creatures of habit. If, in the past, someone provided us with good information, they go onto our list of well-informed people. That also explains why, on the Internet, Web sites with comparative information are very popular. Other people's opinions do count.

This *principle of least effort*[11] was discovered as early as halfway through the 20th century. Anyone taking a closer look at organizations knows that many people still take this as their starting point—and that's not necessarily a bad thing.

Regarding this laziness in the search for information, other elements are also of importance, such as cultural influences, cost-benefit analyses, and the physical situation of the inquirer. Someone looking for directions in a strange town often asks a random passerby. This citizen does not just provide the required information, but often volunteers some extra detail on his town. Some even walk along for part of the way. Why do people share this knowledge? On the surface of it, it does not bring them anything. Nevertheless, a smile or a word of thanks from the stranger seems to be enough payment for sharing this knowledge. You expect the same when you need directions.

Serendipity

It has happened to us all, a situation where you come across information that you were not seeking. Even stronger, many news items exist merely by the grace of this sort of information, as well as our inborn curiosity. We call this *serendipity*, the gift for accidentally and intelligently finding something we were not actively seeking. This aspect plays an important role in our information behavior. As you surf the Internet, walk across town, read headlines, eavesdrop, browse a bookstore—you pick up information by accident in many places and events, though you are not consciously looking for it. When this accidental information is of personal interest to us, it arouses our curiosity, and we will very quickly make it our own.

Search engines provide a lot of accidental information. We find Web sites we did not know existed and come across useful information gathered by like-minded people. Our colleagues, family, and friends also often volunteer interesting information.

You can control all these coincidences. After all, you decide all day long which information "accidentally" comes your way, because you choose to see or not see certain people, and you decide whether to consult certain information sources or not. When reading your favorite periodical, you come across a story that interests you very much. That is, of course, is not a coincidence. You can therefore control coincidences by selecting the right information sources. You can also make sure that you or your knowledge are found, for example, by creating a profile for yourself as a speaker at conferences, using Web 2.0 tools such as blogs and Twitter, or simply by telling people what you know and are capable of accomplishing.

CONCLUSION

In the first four chapters, we have seen that information is linked with people in particular. Only people are able to turn information into knowledge and wisdom. This takes place in their own brain and is therefore a personal activity. Nobody else can determine the true value of information to you.

It follows that the sense of too much information is mainly a perception of one's personal situation. We can supply people with all kinds of modern IT resources that provide exactly the right information. We can train our memory. We can learn how to better remember and retrieve information. We can provide people with external aids, such as diaries, computers, and other people, or internal memory strategies, such as creating mnemonic aids and visualization techniques, for example. However, ultimately there is only one person who can change your information behavior: Only you have access to the space between your ears.

If you have read this book in order, you can do the same with Part II. However, try starting by carefully browsing through Part II. Make a note of what you will read immediately and what can wait until later. This is an excellent technique. Particularly, read this book just the way you read a newspaper or a periodical: anything that does not interest you, you simply skip.

Use Part II of this book as a weapon in the battle against the large amount of useless information. Teach yourself how to deal with information more effectively. Use your contacts with other people and use them as sources of information. But above all, allow yourself the necessary rest, and be sure to convey it to others. That is ultimately the best way of dealing with information overload and for coping with information more effectively.

NOTES

1. Johnstone, D., Tate, M., & Bonner, M. (2004). Bringing human information behaviour into information systems research: An application of systems modeling. *Information Research*, *9*(4), http://InformationR.net/ir/9−4/paper191.html.
2. Wilson, T. D. (2000). Human information behavior. *Informing Science*, *3*(2), 49−56.
3. Ibid.
4. Bates, M. J. (2005). Berrypicking. In: Fisher, K. E., Erdelez, S., & McKechnie, E. F. (Eds.). *Theories of information behavior: A researcher's guide*. Medford, NJ: Information Today.
5. Savolainen, R. (1995). Everyday life information seeking: Approaching information seeking in the context of "way of life." *Library & Information Science Research*, *17*, 259−294.
6. Pirolli, P. & Card, S. (1999). Information foraging. *Psychological Review*, *106*(4), 634−675.
7. Fisher, K. E. (2005). Information grounds. In: Fisher, K. E., S. Erdelez & E. F. McKechnie (Eds.). *Theories of information behavior: A researcher's guide*. Medford, NJ: Information Today.
8. Marchand, D. A., Kettinger, W. J., & Rollins, J. D. (2001). *Making the invisible visible: How companies win with the right information, people, and IT*. London: John Wiley & Sons.

9. Sonnenwald, D. H. (2005). Information horizons. In: Fisher, K. E., Erdelez, S., & McKechnie, E. F. (Eds.). *Theories of information behavior: A researcher's guide*. Medford, NJ: Information Today.

10. Jones, W. (2008). *Keeping found things found: The study and practice of personal information management*. Amsterdam: Morgan Kaufmann.

11. Case, D. O. (2005). Principle of least effort. In: Fisher, K. E., Erdelez, S., & McKechnie, E. F. (Eds.). *Theories of information behavior: A researcher's guide*. Medford, NJ: Information Today.

PART II

IN PRACTICE

CHAPTER 5

INFORMATION PROFILE

People differ in the way they collect, analyze, and disseminate information. Yet hardly anyone uses this knowledge when they exchange information. When we communicate, regardless of the format, we mainly think about ourselves. Receivers of information do not generally provide feedback to the sender when receiving unwanted information. Such feedback could help the sender disseminate information in more accurate and timely ways in the future.

An information profile serves as an aid to understand a person's information habits. An information profile is a list of a person's information characteristics. It describes a person's aptitude, attitude, and way they handle information. Just as when you describe a person as being, for example, extroverted, action-oriented, or friendly, you can elaborate on how a person deals with information. An information profile also consists of someone's habits when dealing with information.

I would like to state explicitly that it is a good idea to start with self-evaluation. Only when you know what your own information profile is will you be able to properly recognize other people's.

It would be going too far to describe a detailed information profile right now. I will simply indicate the main components.

In an extensive information profile, you will get an answer to the following questions:

- *Attitude.* Can you mentally stand up to the danger of too much information? Are you self-confident and in control of the situation?
- *Decisiveness.* Are you capable of taking decisions on new information quickly and accurately? For example, do you go through all information documents just once, or do you repeat new information a few times?
- *Influence.* Are you capable of influencing others with regard to their information behavior? Do you always lead by example by just passing on necessary information at the right moment?
- *Organization.* Are you capable of properly organizing information? Do you throw information out when necessary? Do you regularly reorganize your archives?
- *Selection.* Are you sufficiently critical for deciding which information you use and which you ignore? Can you establish the right priorities?
- *Skill.* Are you properly capable of handling all IT resources? Do you, for example, know the technical instructions for filtering and selecting?

The actual analysis, with points for improvement, requires professional supervision.

Another option is to compare several people's information profiles, or have them compared, and above all discuss them. Discussion will always add the most value.

An information profile includes the following components:

- Background
- Information aptitude
- Information attitude
- Information handling

A PERSON'S BACKGROUND

An information profile starts with general information on the person, his education, his work experience and other important details. The number of full-time employees (FTEs) who assist the manager directly or indirectly in acquiring, processing, and distributing information is also included. Things such as family, friends, and hobbies are stated. Finally, this section indicates the person's strengths and weaknesses with regard to dealing with information.

Analysis of Information Flows

Next, an analysis is made of the person's information and communication flows. This does not just involve e-mail or reports from IT systems; it also includes the spoken word, reading of books and periodicals during leisure, talking to friends and family. By making a broad inventory, the person finds out exactly what he or she spends time on and which information flows and sources are useful.

One of the methods for making this inventory is drawing up an information report. You can do that with an information report that focuses on the Ws: when, what, who, and why.

- By writing down *when* you need information, you can, for example, find out that you do need news several times per day. Using technical solutions such as RSS, you can satisfy this need with minimal effort.
- By writing down *what* information you need, you can see which information sources recur regularly and how many of these you actually use. It is, for example, possible that your source is a good one, but that you tend to limit yourself to this source too much.
- By writing down *who* you exchange information with, you will find out whether you communicate with the same people all the time.
- By writing down *why* you need information, it may, for example, become clear that you are trying to find information in case of uncertainty or when you have to justify yourself.

Over two to three days, keep a record of which information you receive and what you do with it. Also assess how much time you devote to each information source.

- The number of received and sent e-mails, instant messages, telephone conversations, text messages, voice mails, and conference calls per day
- Hours per day spent on each of these means of communication
- Hours per week spent reading newspapers, journals, articles, and books (business as well as private)
- Hours per week spent on radio, television, and internet (business as well as private)
- Hours per week spent on other sources of information, such as wikis, blogs, music, and videos (business and private)
- Hours per day spent on technologies for processing information

The ultimate purpose of this inventory is to recognize your own personal way of informing and communicating. Only then will you be able to find out where you spend too much time or when it is better for you to use a different type of communication.

IT and Information Competencies

The general part of someone's information profile should also include a description of a person's knowledge and skills regarding the main IT tools and information sources. Everyone knows that it takes time to learn new technologies. Additionally, you as well as most of your colleagues are receiving relatively little training in information skills; it is assumed that they will manage. Acknowledging a lack of practical skills is the first step for better dealing with information.

Personality

When talking about the way in which we share, remember, and distribute information, we cannot ignore our personalities. Heinström[1] convincingly demonstrated that personal styles influence people's information behavior. In the following list, I will provide a possible classification for making an inventory of a person's personal style with regard to information behavior.

- *Extroversion-introversion.* An extroverted person has an adventurous, assertive, and free attitude toward information and enjoys listening to his or her own voice. An introverted person, however, prefers to keep information to him- or herself, or in any case, does not advertise it. Extroverts do indeed easily acquire a lot of the right information, but that does not necessarily mean they also use it correctly. They would rather spend time on other people; after all, that is what they are good at.
- *Agreeableness.* People characterized by this word gladly provide information and are altruistic and caring. They have an ability to empathize with others.
- *Conscientiousness.* These people are goal-oriented and wish to achieve something by supplying information. They are often proficient, neat, conscientious, and reliable and have a large sense of responsibility. They have properly organized their information and information sources. These focused persons do not just collect valuable information; they also use it well in their analyses and decisions.
- *Neuroticism.* This description perhaps has negative undertones, but by this I refer to persons who are nervous or very emotional. They often supply information that is incomplete or information with a strong personal, and therefore subjective, element. They strongly react to information stimuli from their environment, often just a little too violently. Neurotic people also have more trouble dealing with conflicting information. In that case, they will ignore part of the information to obtain a better sense of control.
- *Openness.* Persons bearing this characteristic are open to new ideas, cultures, views, or interests and are willing to share this information with others. Being open to new information is especially important during the first phase of searching for information. This is why we notice that these people, who are very curious and critical by nature, discover a lot of information by accident. They also dare to ask questions, which is a precondition for obtaining good information.

There are countless personality tests on the Internet. Of course, the results of these tests do not explain everything. However, people's personalities are, over time, relatively stable. It follows that this is also the case with their information behavior. As a result, changes to that behavior are very gradual. From one day to the next, you cannot force someone to start sharing information they have carefully accumulated over a long period.

INFORMATION APTITUDE

Information aptitude refers to one's inherent ability for learning, understanding, or performing with information. A person's aptitude with information is given at birth, although it changes throughout his or her life with the acquisition of information skills and other capabilities. Just like the next two sections, information attitude and information handling, the list provided here is not exhaustive. Where necessary, I will include a brief explanation in each section. However, this is certainly not comprehensive. It is just an indication of the things you need to consider.

Readers versus Listeners

Evidence shows that 70 percent of all people are readers, whereas the remaining 30 percent like to receive or transmit information verbally. If you collect a lot of information, more often than not you are a reader. A listener prefers vocal communication, preferably combined with a physical meeting. Less than 5 percent of all people also have a preference for including some form of tactile communication: they need to literally "feel" the object or person. Of course, these preferences also depend on the type of medium, the content of the message, timing aspects, and the like.

Readers want reports followed by discussion; listeners want exactly the opposite. If you know the other person's preference upfront, you can use the most effective means of communication. You can send an e-mail to a listener, but a face-to-face meeting with that person will be far more effective. Typically, the higher you rise in an organization, the more you will see managers that are listeners. When talking about a good CEO, most people would agree that he or she is a good listener. That is what leadership is all about: listening carefully to all the pros and cons and then making an informed decision.

Most people are both readers and listeners. They normally do both at the same time: taking notes and listening to a presentation, for example. That is a good thing: the more cues a person gets and the more senses are addressed, the better they retain new information in their memory and have it available for recall.

Speakers versus Writers

Just as there is a way in which people receive information, there is also a preference for transferring information, either by word of mouth or in writing. We all know people who tell us something during a meeting and then at the end add: "I will send you an e-mail." In this case, the distinction of course is not one thing or the other. But if you know that you personally prefer putting something on paper, then your environment can better take this into account. Otherwise, why would some managers never react to that e-mail?

Verbalizer versus Imager

There is another distinction in sending information—namely, someone's preference for expressing their thoughts in words or in pictures. Techniques such as mind-mapping are wasted on wordsmiths. Some managers, certainly those of the new, younger generation, swear by visual material (particularly with movement). This approach goes even further. Entire manuals are presented via online videos. Important meetings are saved and at a later stage replayed as an asynchronous and (where necessary) sped up Webcast.

Five Senses

Our senses are continuously exposed to all kinds of information. We do not really know why people experience the information they receive through their five senses that differently. But also try and look at it from the recipient's perspective. By using words, we are able to transfer feelings, ideas, and opinions, hoping to evoke an identical experience in others. However, the recipient usually has an entirely different frame of reference than the sender. This means that some words may be interpreted entirely differently than originally intended.

Most of us are born with a preference for visual information, so access to a visual display of information helps everyone to receive and understand information better. However, we have to take these statistics into account: on average, we remember 20 percent of what we read, 30 percent of what we hear, 40 percent of what we see, 50 percent of what we say, and 60 percent of what we do—but we remember as much as 90 percent of what we see, hear, say, *and* do.

Pilers versus Filers

People use an array of strategies to organize all their information sources. A large number of people rely on visual displays and cues. For them, the motto "out of sight, out of mind" applies. They accumulate huge piles of documents, books, and magazines on their desk, which at first sight might seem chaotic. They also have a seemingly cluttered desktop with numerous links. These users are referred to as *pilers*. They work best by keeping their work in sight. When they see a pile, it helps them remember what is in it. Keeping their work visible also helps them keeping track of what they have to do.

Filers, however, like to structure their life by putting items of information away in an organized manner in neat closets or electronic systems. They work best when their desktop and inbox are clear of everything except what they are currently working on. What is on top of their desks provides focus to them; clutter distracts them. They keep things they are not currently working on out of sight, relying on alphabetical, numerical, or other ordering systems to keep track.

Both styles—filing and piling—help people mentally organize their time, tasks, and materials. Each style calls for a different type of workspace design. A filer is aimed at "finding," a piler at "reminding."

Filers often experience the frustration of not being able to find things once they have been filed. Most filers, therefore, have to go through the tedious process of re-categorization and maintenance. Filers have two problems finding stuff: They tend to file too much because they have put so much effort into building a filing system, and they often find it hard to remember how they categorized things. Fortunately, desktop search systems can help them with their electronic archive, at least.

However, people do not always fit in the either-or scheme. Both methods of organization are effective. Problems do not arise unless you try to force a structure on someone else or when you start using joint working spaces (including electronic ones). Recognition of someone's organizational preference is the first step toward better use of information.

Global versus Detail

Some people wish to know everything in detail; others settle for an overview with aggregated data or an overview of deviations from the set standard. Occasionally, a manager will go further and tell his team members that he just wants to be informed when they cannot work things out for themselves. In passing, he adds that they need to have thought of at least two solutions already. It's the ultimate way of delegating.

Learning Styles

How people learn new information depends on the way their particular brain learns. Each person has a different learning style. A useful theory does not take the incoming information into account, but the way people assimilate information once they receive it.[2]

We can identify four styles of learning:

1. *Activist.* For the activist, learning has to be fun. "What can you actively do with this information?" this person asks him- or herself, time and time again. Activists love discussion and new ideas, but they avoid detail and often do not complete assignments. Particularly allow activists to lead meetings or brief brainstorming sessions, for example, or arrive at solutions by means of role play or other games.

2. *Reflector.* A reflector is someone who prefers looking at information from several perspectives before acquiring it. His or her opinion is always considered and well-phrased. A reflector is strongly analytical in character. Allow reflectors time to process information, and certainly do not give them the leading role in projects.

3. *Theorist.* This is someone who stores information with his or her existing knowledge. A theorist is purposeful, collects as much objective information as possible, and supplies others with clear instructions. Therefore, a theorist should be presented with new information gradually and in a logical order.

4. *Pragmatist.* This person likes to know how he or she can use new information. A pragmatist is practical, fairly impatient, and dislikes superfluous information. A pragmatist does not have time for abstract or theoretical discussion. Be sure to always fit in information with the pragmatist's mental model.

INFORMATION ATTITUDE

Information attitude refers to the positive or negative views a person has toward information. A person's attitude influences his or her behavior and changes his or her experience with, in this case, information use.

Information Junkie

This refers to a person's curiosity for information. Some people only collect information for the information itself. They are never satisfied, even though they know that most of the information they acquire is useless. If they could only figure out which 5 percent of the information was really worth having! Newsstands, CNN, RSS feeds, coffee corners: Nothing can satisfy their immense hunger for information.

Some of us complain about too much useless information. Information junkies won't, as they need to be "in the know." They collect information just for fun, for a sense of control, to learn, to influence other people, or to get a head start.

It is not surprising that most people start their working day by exchanging information to be "informed." They go for a morning coffee at the coffee corner, check their e-mails and voice mails, socialize and gossip with their peers, or share stories about what happened last night or over the weekend. Most people agree that *not* having the latest piece of information is far more intimidating than running the risk of too much useless information.

Knowing What You Have to Know

Many information workers are struggling with the dilemma: "What do I have to know, and how do I know I have to know it?" They ask this question about almost every information source. It is increasingly difficult to stay on top of the mountain of information needed to perform tasks at work.

Asking the right questions is becoming a key capability in our society. We are becoming answer-rich, but question-poor. If you ask yourself two questions ("quest for information") on a regular basis, Drucker[3] contends that your work will become very effective. These questions are:

1. What information do I owe to the people with whom I work and on whom I depend? In what form? And in what time frame?
2. What information do I need myself? From whom? In what form? And in what time frame?

The first question gives direction to where your attention should go, whereas the second one deals with the activities needed for answering the first question. This will obviously result in less information being handled and therefore prevent feelings of information overload. By limiting yourself to a short list of issues and concepts that you need to know in detail, you can ignore much of the information around you. Simply ignore some of the information and focus. Focusing means learning what to ignore.

Your information profile should state what your attitude to knowledge is. Better even, your main areas of expertise and interest can be part of your profile.

Uncertainty

A person never has all the information he needs to make an *informed* decision. But often, far less information than he thinks is needed to make a *good* decision. The final 20 percent of required information often takes too much time and effort to acquire and does not add significant value.

Loss of control over information is the single most important symptom of feelings of information overload. This means that one has to let go. In today's environment, where there is too much information available, one has to do something counterintuitive: Limit the amount of information you study before you make your decision. There simply isn't enough time; you cannot afford the luxury of studying every word on the issue and reaching 100 percent certainty on a decision.

This part of someone's profile states whether someone has the capability of ceasing his search for yet more information on time. It also describes whether such a person is capable of making a decision in spite of the fact that he lacks *crucial* information or does not receive it in time.

Ignorance

People do not know what they don't know. Paradoxically, some people want to know everything on a certain subject. They simply cannot abide for others to know more than they do. However, the more they know on a specific subject, the more they realize that they do not know everything yet. That has to be frustrating, because it is simply impossible to know all there is to know on any given subject.

First, there is so much information on the subject in question that there is simply not enough time to take it all in. After all, some information can only be experienced physically: What would it be like to climb a high mountain or to be on the stage during the Oscar® ceremony?

Second, the limits of a chosen subject are vague by definition. Suppose that someone wishes to know everything about high mountains. What, in that case, is a high mountain exactly? Does he wish to climb them all as well? Where are his limitations?

Suppose everyone helps that person in finding out all there is to know on that one subject. Then he will have to face a third limitation: His memory may be big enough, but it is utopian to think that he can store all this information properly and accessibly, as well as being able to recall it all at a later date. In particular, the access to specific information in our memory often presents a problem.

In spite of that, many people continue to collect information. It is not in our nature to admit to not knowing something. How often does it happen that you should really admit that you don't know, but you do not actually say it? Feelings of guilt can never be the cause, because everybody has this same problem. Furthermore, stating that you don't know something allows you to learn from others who do. Admitting to not knowing everything and not having to know everything is quite a relief. Acknowledging your ignorance is an ideal basis for learning things.

In an information profile, a person should also define the subjects he definitely does *not* wish to be informed on.

INFORMATION HANDLING

Information handling refers to ways a person deals with information in his or her day-to-day activities. Obviously, how someone manages and uses information is in addition to his or her personal traits, attitudes, and beliefs toward information.

Personal Information Management

In Chapter 2, we saw that people have extensive information collections for all sorts of reasons. Those personal information collections are an important part of a your information profile. The description should include the place, reason, overall contents, and the way in which these collections are accessed. As seen earlier in this chapter, you can make an inventory of these collections by means of an information report. All these collections are the first source that you consult when seeking information. I need to rectify that last remark—of course, the very first source is your own digital memory, your brain.

Information Organization

Filing acquired information has become a major part of your work. However, you have not been trained to file large quantities of different types of information properly. But you can learn this. For digital documents, you do not need to make as much of an effort, particularly when you search smartly on your desktop or shared working spaces.

Also included in the information profile is your organization of the information. This is not about folder structures or the alphabetical setup of your customer database. This is about the basic principles of the management of information: which information is stored where and in which form. There is no such thing as a best way when it comes to arranging information. But no matter how it is arranged, two principles remain applicable. You have to be able to explain this classification quickly to someone else, and you should also regularly check whether the chosen classification is still workable.

As increasingly more people work in *virtual* teams, these classifications are an absolute necessity. After all, wouldn't it be nice to know how the other person prefers to see information presented and how he or she prefers to communicate with you?

Filtering

An effective way of dealing with a large amount of information properly is setting filters. Filters are techniques for letting through only important information systematically. They consist of technical filters, such as in e-mail systems, but it is also possible to include filters in our communication. In fact, this happens more often than we think. Every reaction to another person is an indication of what you want to hear or not hear during the rest of the conversation. Furthermore, as senders, we often only provide the information that we expect to be important to the receiver. Filters prime our thinking and test whether new information is important.

Your information profile will state which filters are set for the main information sources, which criteria you're using, and especially how often these filters are attended to. Do not forget that I mean all types of filters, so you should also communicate your preference to the people around you. A practical example explains this.

Many managers have a secretary or personal assistant who often takes over a large part of the managers' administrative tasks. Yet, the communication between these people assumes implicit presumptions. They seldom check whether the requirements, demands, and expectation are still up-to-date. At one time, I asked a member of the Board of Directors, "How often do you agree with your secretary on which criteria she is to use for allowing information to reach you?" He immediately understood the purpose of my question. At my next visit, the secretary thanked me. Presently, they each know better which information they both really needed for their work.

However, do not forget that filters that are too rigid exclude coincidences. You will no longer accidentally stumble across information, as is often part of searches on the Internet. You must weigh the pros and cons between receiving a large amount of information and receiving the right information.

Information Pruning

Just for the fun of it, track for a whole day where all information belongs: "need-to-know" or "nice-to-know." As regards the first information flow, it is important to prune. Which information can you really do without and still make good decisions? As regards the second information flow, you can decide more quickly to simply stop receiving it. You will not miss out on anything, as you do not use this information for decisions but often just to be able to join in conversations. Besides, this superfluous information leaves you less time for really important information.

It is also possible to prune automatically. When setting up a new information source, you immediately indicate its expiry date and which action should take place at that date: ask for renewal, file, or cancel.

It is important for the information profile to set aside time and capacity for this pruning activity. By time, I simply mean to say whether you, for example, have planned one hour per week for maintenance on your information sources. By capacity, I mean whether you need any help (e.g., a professional organizer) or an additional course (setting filters and other technical measures), or that reports and the like from information systems need to be set up better and whether other people d need to be towhy particular information is no longer required.

Time Management

Time is a unique resource. One cannot rent, hire, buy, or otherwise obtain more time. Time is always in exceedingly short supply. The advantage is that no one person has more time than another. If, however, you manage your time properly, you will see that you can have more useable time.

Most people like to have large chunks of time to dedicate to information tasks. Certainly, when working with information, you rarely have the ability to handle more than one large, demanding information task simultaneously. Moreover, frequent changing between these different information tasks means continuously keeping track of where you are and, as a result, rereading things you previously read in order to catch up. By having large amounts of time available for information tasks, you can be more productive.

Attention and concentration are controlled by the prefrontal cortex, the executive manager of your brain. This manager is only able to do one single task at a time. Each disruption, no matter how small, leads to light stress and a sense of being pressed for time. In an environment with a lot of information, we can easily lose the ability to plan and organize our own affairs. This results in managers concentrating on information they already know and that seems attractive—not always the best choice.

Just as an information report shows you all of the information sources you use, the first requisite for better information behavior is insight into the way you spend your time. In your information profile, you record how much time you spend on each of the main sources from that information report. You keep this record for a set period. Next, you analyze whether the actual time spent corresponds with your expectations. Differences may result in adjustment of the norm, the use of different information sources, or simple acceptance of the fact that things sometimes take up more time.

To-Do Lists

Human memory is notoriously faulty. Very few people can juggle all their tasks in their head. We constantly forget important dates, meetings, names, and the proverbial car keys. It is probably safe to predict that this situation is only going to get worse. Our world is becoming more complicated and information-driven, and our memory is not improving.

Because you need to remember increasingly more, you are in need of an aid: a list of actions. It does not matter how you record this— sticky notes, a BlackBerry, your e-mail system, or a special "To-Do" folder. The system you use is fixed in your information profile. In the next chapters of the book, you will learn how to manage these lists practically.

In an information profile, you record which lists the person uses for keeping up with activities. Especially for managers, this profile also has to include the lists of their supporting employees. Each list clearly states who registers things in it, who maintains it, and where the *original* list is laid down.

From my own practical experience, I can say that this exercise alone will mean a lot of added value for many managers. I also advise you to draw up a list of subjects that you are not interested in—a "not-to-do" list.

CONCLUSION

A important step in effective information behavior is to know yourself. Who else knows your information profile best? For example, do you know how much information you receive per medium, how much time you spend per medium, and whether you are using the right technology in the most effective way? If change is needed, you will have to be familiar with your own way of working and how it could be improved. To have maximum impact as information senders, you should know as much about the information profiles of your audiences as you do about your own profiles.

An information profile is, of course, a snapshot. Your environment changes, often faster than you think. External factors such as time and money mean that you need to be continuously attentive to your information behavior and how you affect others with it. Furthermore, knowing your profile means that you will also be able to give attention to the right things. This does not yield just money but also prestige, trust, speed of action, and a more pleasant life.

There is also nothing wrong with telling your colleagues why you would rather discuss certain subjects in a conversation rather than via e-mail. Also, tell them where you file your own information and your business information. Tell those close to you why you have these paper mountains in your room or working space, or why you immediately file everything. There are no wrongs or rights; at worst, things are different from what others expect.

Also, discuss your information profile with three people: your boss (the person who is responsible for your salary or the person that gives you assignments), a trusted colleague of a different department (someone with whom you do not have a real working relationship), and someone from your circle of relatives or friends (someone from whom you can take negative remarks). Do something with their comments, and offer to be a sounding board to them as well. In any case, revise this profile on a yearly basis, and take action if you really wish to improve yourself.

Smart managers do not know just their own information profiles. They also have a clear idea of the information profiles of the most important people in their environment and of the group profiles of their interest groups. To have the greatest possible influence and action orientation on the receiver of their message, this insight is vital.

NOTES

1. Heinström, J. (2003). Five personality dimensions and their influence on information behaviour. *Information Research, 9*(1), http://informationr. net/ir/9-1/paper165.html.
2. Hale-Evans, R. (2006). *Mind performance hacks: Tips & tools for overclocking your brain.* Sebastopol, CA: O'Reilly Media.
3. Drucker, P. F. (1999). *Management challenges for the 21st century.* Oxford: Butterworth-Heinemann.

CHAPTER 6

MIND YOUR BRAIN

Our senses are continuously bombarded with all sorts of information-rich bites: billboards, music, other people, and many more information stimuli. We expect our brain to select, remember, and use the right signs from these large amounts of information. In addition, we expect it to properly process all emotional signs.

A computer is powered by electricity, but what food does our brain need in order to perform well? And why do we need to exercise and play games? This chapter shows you why.

SENSITIVE INFORMATION

Our senses collect and our brains filter and organize information every minute of the day. These are definitely information: a drop of water on your elbow, a child's cry far away, the material from which your new dress is made, that smell from your youth that you had forgotten, or that familiar-looking face that you cannot connect to a name.

Olfactory

When we say that we find something delicious, we often mean to say that it smells nice; an important part of taste is determined by smell. Smells are an important source of information. Our nose immediately passes on smell signals to the limbic system, which is part of the mammalian brain. Smells are closely connected to memories. After the 20th year of our life, our sense of smell deteriorates drastically, at a rate of about 50 percent per decade. This probably explains why older people often associate smells with "old" memories. Each time we remember a certain fact, we record this memory in a new interpretation. The memory therefore changes because it is recalled. However, the process is different with smells. Because we add relatively few new smells during our lifetime, we often remember these in their original form.

Smells are a powerful means of communication. However, we can only deploy them to a certain extent, because they require physical presence. It is possible to use the power of smells metaphorically. In cosmetics, free samples are a common marketing method. Similar free samples can also be used when exchanging information. Think of things like reading suggestions, publishing a first chapter of a book on the Internet, asking opening questions prior to a conversation. These are all ways of "sniffing out" the atmosphere in advance.

Enlightenment

In the office and at home, we are usually at our computer in dimly lit and badly ventilated rooms. Artificial light only partly helps; natural light is always best. Good light is one of the preconditions for processing information, just like eating, sleeping, and a well-heated environment, rich in oxygen. Even bright artificial light seems to have an immediate stimulating effect on someone's alertness and performance. If you work for a boss, then you are partly dependent on others as far as your working conditions are concerned. If you have your own workplace, regardless of where this is situated, then you are able to take ergonomic measures in order to ensure sufficient light. In particular, do not forget to go for a walk during your lunch hour!

Laughing Out Loud

We are born with the ability to laugh. A liberating laugh will get you far. Many presentations, parties, or television shows revolve around humor—not just jokes about people and situations, but also plays on words, visual gags, and everyday slips of the tongue. All of these make people laugh. The person telling the joke or the one responsible for the play on words immediately receives feedback. When we are laughing, the brain produces the hormone endorphin, which makes us feel good. Furthermore, endorphin has a calming effect and relieves pain. Because a joke often makes us feel good, we remember the emotional context of the exchanged information better.

Through laughing, you also become more flexible. An unexpected twist can breach certain expectations and force you to reinterpret all previously received information. Humor is an excellent way to change your perspective on certain situations. When our brain receives information that is presented with humor, it switches very quickly from one state to another. We recognize a new perspective, and we laugh about it. It makes us more social as well as smarter, and it allows us to better react to unexpected situations.

Humor can raise a smile or remove tension, but it does a lot more than that. Word jokers, for example, teach us subtle differentiations in our language. Humor teaches us to improve our ability to express ourselves and thereby better communicate a message to the recipient.

Laughing also demonstrates that someone feels safe. After all, they are directly showing their most profound emotions. As a result, laughing is a predominantly social activity. The chances of laughing in the company of others are 30 times larger than when you are on your own. Speakers, in fact, laugh more often than their audience. Laughing is contagious!

Women laugh more often than men—and what's more, they laugh more heartily and more contagiously. Women know that laughing reduces stress and pain, boosts their confidence and defense mechanisms, and can improve their social life. Humor is always in their top three qualities that the ideal partner should have. Many employers also appreciate employees with a sense of humor. A cheerful person performs better and is even offered better jobs.

Music, Maestro

Music has unique characteristics. We do not have to make an effort to remember a song; it seems to happen without any effort. Music and language are each other's counterparts. The left half of our brain is mainly language oriented; the right half is more into music. Music releases powerful emotions in us and creates strong connections in our brain. The song we shared with our sweetheart, our first concert, a ballad that was especially written for us. Music mainly relates to our autobiographical memory. Music is narrative. Our brain is also very sensitive to certain musical qualities, such as melody and rhythm. Music often makes us feel good. No wonder it plays such an important part in media such as television and film.

We prefer to listen to music that fits with the rhythm of our brain. When we are young, we like fast beats. As we get older, we start to appreciate different kinds of music. It is just the same with information. As we get older, we need less information. Although we do not read any more slowly, we do start to process information at a slower rate after our 39th year. Moreover, we simply do not need all this information; we know by now that it will no longer improve our life.

The fact that we remember music quickly is demonstrated by the fact that we only need to hear a few notes of a certain tune before recognizing the song. This especially applies to hit records or evergreens; songs that are often repeated are indelibly printed in our memory. In other words, do occasionally use music for making sure that the message comes across and is remembered.

Sleep Well

"Sleep on it," we often say. After a good night's sleep, some problems do not seem half as bad. That sleep has a restoring effect is a well-known fact. The hippocampus plays the information we have received during the day one more time, mixes it with previous experiences, and stores the memory again. If the brain processed this information during the day, then it would also have to process all new sensory stimuli simultaneously.

Especially after a day of many new impressions, a good night's sleep is very important. Your brain needs the time to process all those new impressions; therefore, sleeping is not a waste of time. For that reason, sleeping is better than endless repetition. During sleep, the procedural memory in particular is active. This memory chiefly decides how we do certain things. By training your brain properly during the day, it is able to continue practicing during the night.

For some people, four hours of sleep is sufficient. Margaret Thatcher and Winston Churchill, for example, were known for just needing a few hours of sleep. Other people swear by an afternoon nap. Leonardo da Vinci had 15 minutes of shuteye every four hours. In other words, he only slept 90 minutes in 24 hours, and this meant he had six extra hours for working and relaxing.

Powernaps, sleeping for a maximum of 20 minutes several times a day, are becoming increasingly popular, also among business people. The long-term effects of these naps still need to be researched. We can catch up on sleep, but it is also possible to sleep "in advance." When we take a nap during the day, it has an effect on our perception of time. At night, we will, for example, go to sleep later.

Allow your brain to really work during the night. The subconscious has plenty of time to think about your problems. So it is a good idea to study that particular issue, read it through once more during the evening, or play it in your mind. Next, do something totally different: Go to sleep and you wake up with the solution, often.

MIXED FEELINGS

In Chapter 3, we saw that feelings influence the processing of information. You can use those basic emotions and characteristics of the brain to handle information in a smarter way.

Emotions as Information

Remembering and recalling is a lot easier when these tasks involve personal emotions. Chapter 3 discussed how emotions such as fear are powerful survival mechanisms, thanks to the amygdala. Our memory improves vastly when we have a strongly emotional experience right after processing information. After studying an important report, for example, allow yourself to see an episode of your favorite comedy, a horror movie, or a few funny videos on YouTube.

Men and women handle emotions differently. From a young age, women seem to be trained for reading facial expressions, interpreting intonations, and picking up other people's unspoken signals. Why are women that good at picking up other people's emotions? Because in women, the amygdala, which is the main brain center in the emotional brain, is activated more quickly. Therefore, many women are able to recall in great detail both pleasant and unpleasant situations many years on.

In today's education, the fact that emotional stimuli are needed for better understanding teaching material is taken into account. In the past, you had to sit still in the classroom. These days, an active position, lots of movement and sharing of personal experiences are in fact welcomed. Theory is alternated with practical exercises, preferably in a small group. Group discussions and other forms of social communication ensure that information is highlighted by emotion.

The Intuitive Mind

Sometimes people claim to know something, without knowing how or why. This feeling is known as intuition. Intuition takes place in our subconscious. In fact, a lot of information reaches us subconsciously. Actions such as driving a car and breathing do not require concentrated thinking. Only when we arrive at an unexpected or unknown situation do we become aware of this. For example, when you meet a new business relation, it immediately feels right . . . or exactly the opposite. Our decisions and judgments are always based on a combination of reason and feelings. The more information we need to process, the more chance that we will make a decision on the basis of our feelings.

Some people argue that you do not need to make important decisions rationally. It is better to decide intuitively on a new house, a different job, or whether or not you should break off your relationship. When asked how they came to a decision, many people answer: "It just felt right" or "I just knew I was doing the right thing." However, intuition is mainly based on experience of life and knowledge. An experienced firefighter knows instinctively whether he should or should not enter a burning building. A younger firefighter, however, will not have sufficient experience for making such a decision.

The phenomenon of intuition can be explained in two ways. The first explanation assumes that over the course of time, we have developed a fast method for making decisions—a shortcut, as it were. The second explanation presumes acquired associations. When we have to form an opinion, our previous experiences play an important part. We will sooner trust a person who has proved to be reliable in the past in one particular area in other areas as well, without being able to really substantiate this. Our first impressions of other people are therefore little more than intuitive opinions.

By "reading minds"—in other words, using our intuition—we are able to assess other people's thoughts, beliefs, and intentions on the basis of minimal clues. We are using nonverbal information to find out someone's intentions. It is not easy to learn mind-reading, even though everybody can do it. We sometimes sense what people wish to achieve when they provide us with information, even without being told explicitly. We can read it in their faces, hear it in their voices, and see it in their body language.

Information Stress

Our brain is geared to changes. It also explains why boredom leads to fatigue, stress, and illness. Most people need the pressure of time, deadlines, and slightly too long lists of activities to function well. Our brain can easily handle this.

Stress, particularly information stress, occurs when we are under constant pressure to incessantly receive, process, and disseminate information and do not have the opportunity to fit in some rest between two stressful situations. Which situations are stressful differs per person.

The symptoms of information stress are obvious. Our attention slackens and we are sidetracked, we cannot finish anything anymore, we read and do not fully understand the information any more, we unjustly snap at people, lose our patience, become restless and fickle, and so on and so forth. Stress reduces the functioning of our memory because it causes the production of the hormone cortisol in high concentrations. Cortisol destroys glucose, the only source of energy for the brain.

In the past, stress was a survival mechanism. It prepared our body for fight or flight. As soon as the danger was over, the body was able to calm down. These days, many people are unable to create these breathers for themselves, so their bodies remain in the state of stress. In and of itself, stress is not harmful. It becomes harmful when the body is not given a chance to restore. Oddly enough, these days it is possible to suffer from information stress even without having to process a vast amount of information. The reason is that we often wrongly assess the future. When we expect information and perhaps do not receive this, then this in itself is sufficient to induce stress.

Research shows that for one-third of us, stress is genetically determined: It runs in the family. The remainder of our stress is explained by the degree of control we have over our life, our choices, and our work. The more we are in control, the less stress we have. This also explains why executives and managers experience less stress, in spite of their busy work. They carry out their work independently and, moreover, have collected a number of people around them who take work off their hands. In addition to their work, managers are intrinsically and, via ample rewards, extrinsically appreciated.

Take your time, and go over the following points to see whether you recognize yourself in these. Identification and recognition are often the best reason for acting on a situation that includes a lot of information stress.

- *Addiction*. Some people are simply addicted to information. In the past, they used to watch CNN 20 times a day; nowadays they often use automatic RSS feeds for keeping continuously informed.
- *Creative*. It may seem strange, but the most creative and innovative thinkers among us more often have the feeling of not having enough time, especially because they are busy working on all sorts of new ideas and innovations.
- *Forgetfulness*. When we are distracted, we often quickly forget what we were doing in the first place.
- *Free spirits*. Not everyone wishes to work within a straitjacket of rules and regulations. However, these free spirits do forget that smart people carefully considered the procedures to be followed. It takes less time when you just follow the rules.
- *Multitasking*. In many work situations, we are simultaneously presented with a mountain of tasks. That is not a problem provided that we actually complete these tasks sometime. But completion is often the problem. The pile of work is forever increasing, and giving us increasingly more pressure. Yet it often takes little effort to check off tasks, one by one.

- *Postponement behavior.* Chronic postponement of tasks leads to work piling up just before the agreed deadline.
- *Pressure.* Some people are very capable of working under pressure. In fact, they *need* to feel that pressure; otherwise, they do not perform. When they are not busy, they remedy this lack of stress by taking on many extra tasks. As a result, information stress automatically occurs.

Do As I Do

Our entire life is spent copying other people's behavior. Children learn from their parents and from each other. Thanks to mirror neurons, we can learn very well just by looking. These neurons also enable us to anticipate situations. Because of this ability, we can empathize with the emotions and intentions of other people. This is in fact a powerful mechanism in human evolution for efficiently transferring information between people without too much interference.

We do not just imitate in order to teach ourselves new things. Imitation also enables us to better collaborate with others. We seem to automatically copy other people's movements when we are with them. That inspires confidence. When people do not imitate our movements, we feel uncomfortable in their company. So when you imitate someone consciously, but as inconspicuously as possible, there is every chance that this person likes you. Apart from gestures, we also copy posture, facial expressions, words, vocabulary, and intonation. Imitating others proves useful during our social interactions. We can try to stop ourselves from doing this, but it would take a lot of effort.

People learn to copy others' examples. So, if you wish to teach someone an action, simply demonstrate the action as often as necessary. Show, for example, where certain information can be found and what you can do with it. Demonstrating and explaining what you are doing are the most powerful methods for using information properly.

FOOD FOR THOUGHT

Ultimately, the brain is a combination of chemical reactions and electrical signals. One person is brighter than the next. You could say that whiz-kids have a better functioning chemical system. If we knew exactly why this is the case, we could use that knowledge for improving other people's brains. For the time being, the main method for achieving this is healthy nutrition.

Brain Chemicals

Our brains can produce their own drugs. I am talking of neurotransmitters, molecules that play a role in the transfer of stimuli between the neurons. One type of neurotransmitter is dopamine, a chemical substance that makes us feel good and affects our time perception. Dopamine is also linked to the award system of the brain. When we achieve a goal, the brain produces dopamine, which makes us feel good. Dopamine can also be produced by any other drug. It is destroyed by Parkinson's disease, and mental illnesses disturb its production.

The substance oxytocin plays an important part when we are in love. It promotes social ties, such as the tie between parents and their children. Oxytocin is also known as the cuddle hormone, because it increases our trust in other people. In stressful and scary situations, women produce more oxytocin, which makes them caring and socially minded. This partly explains why women are more geared to social interactions than men. The oxytocin hormone makes women feel better more quickly after moments of stress, both mentally as well as physically. The hormone also seems to have an effect on the hippocampus that improves our memory and learning ability. In a nutshell, dopamine causes excitement, and oxytocin provides rest, calm, and trust.

Another neurotransmitter is serotonin. This substance regulates the irritability of cells or, as an expert phrased nicely: "Serotonin is one of the molecules in the orchestra, but it is the molecule that beats time." Serotonin is involved in many processes; for example, it plays roles in learning, sleeping, fear, and stress. If you, as a manager, pay real attention to your workers and really support them, they receive an extra dose of serotonin. A lack of serotonin can lead to depression, irritability, listlessness, headaches, unrestrained appetite, or no appetite at all.

We humans are curious and have a penchant for new things. That curiosity is crucial to our functioning. Research shows that our brain includes a separate neurochemical system for recognizing new experiences and surprises. This system in particular is to a large degree regulated by the production of dopamine. Dopamine controls our working memory. The brain cells of that memory focus all their attention on strong stimuli and active goals, instead of distracting stimuli. That is why it is important to ensure that the information you offer is unique and eye-catching.

Besides, dopamine plays an important part in most cognitive and emotional functions. If dopamine levels are high, we are in a cheerful mood and perform better. It is even true that the older we are, the more important the relation between our mood and learning ability becomes. This is because with age, the sensitivity of our brain decreases. In that case, a minor increase in the dopamine level has a relatively major effect. In other words, make sure to be happy or stay happy when you have to process information.

Brain Food

Glucose is one of the main fuels of our brain; it is produced by our body from different types of sugar. That explains why we like cola, candy, and cakes. Glucose can be absorbed directly by the blood, and it quickly reaches the brain. As opposed to the other cells in our body, brain cells are unable to convert fat or protein into glucose. The brain is also unable to store glucose like the muscles do. For that reason, it is important to our brain to take in food equally divided over the entire day.

When we sleep, we lose consciousness. That does not mean to say that our brain is also resting. Brains never sleep. Our brain also consumes energy during the night. This means that it needs extra energy (i.e., glucose) in the morning. The only way of getting that energy is a hearty breakfast. Remember the old saying: "Eat breakfast like a king, eat lunch like a prince, and eat dinner like a beggar." This is dietary advice in a nutshell, but with a large element of truth. Be sure to have a hearty breakfast, do not have too heavy a lunch, and go for a light hot meal in the evening. By having three healthy meals a day, you are sure to take in all the nutrients that your body needs. Apart from sufficient liquids, you must make sure that you get enough carbohydrates, fat, fibers, vitamins, and minerals.

Our brain uses almost a quarter of all the energy we take in. To be able to learn well, concentrate, recall, have sufficient energy, and maintain a pleasant mood, we require proper nourishment. Certain foods, such as salmon, herring, crustaceans, shellfish, and eggs assist us in this. Experts also recommend eating a lot of fresh fruit, vegetables, nuts, and raisins.

Food Advice

It is essential to make sure that we eat the right foods. Many problems with concentration and problems in processing large amounts of information are created by wrong eating habits. Some food tips that will benefit your brain:

- Drink a lot of water. By regularly drinking water, you promote the intake of glucose in your blood and thus the energy supply to your brain, your own information factory.
- Your glucose levels should be as stable as possible. For the supply of energy to the brain, you should ideally have a meal three times a day and a maximum of three light snacks.
- If you do not eat or eat little over a long period of time, your body has to produce special enzymes. That requires a lot of energy, which strongly reduces your concentration over a period of time.
- For using the glucose from your blood, the brain needs oxygen. That is why an environment with lots of fresh air is good for you.
- Cholesterol is not bad for the brain. On the contrary, the brain itself produces cholesterol. You need this substance for being able to learn well.
- Fatty fish is good for you. These types of fish contain omega-3 fatty acids, which are vital to your brainpower and to being able to better deal with stress.
- Drink coffee, but in moderation. Studies show that we remember information better and that our memory improves when we drink a few cups of coffee a day.
- On average, it takes 20 minutes from the time we swallow food until we get the signal that tells us we have had enough. It is therefore better to chew well and eat at a slower pace. The same goes, in fact, for the processing of information. It is a smart idea to take in information slowly. Allow data to slowly sink in, turn

it over in your mind, and work out what else you would like to know. Allow your brain the time to process information.

Finally, the best food tip of all: Enjoy good food together with friends. When we eat together, we take our time. Moreover, we strengthen our bonds with our friends by lingering over the dinner table. During the meal, we exchange information, which might come in useful in our future work or other activities. We remember this information better because we are having a good time and enjoying ourselves. Furthermore, an enjoyable meal will often leave all participants with a positive feeling that may last for days.

BRAIN MUSCLES

It seems strange that you need to exercise more to process information better. However, exercise is more than just a physical activity. It requires that body and mind properly work together. This means that they have to integrate planning, attention, memory, and other motor and cognitive processes with one another. A brisk walk, for example, promotes that integration. Exercise encourages the growth of the number of connections between our brain cells. What's more, by exercising you produce new brain cells and get more energy.

People are true hikers. Our ancestors easily covered ten to twenty miles a day. Remaining seated for eight out of twenty-four hours is a fairly recent development. Regular exercise prevents cognitive distortions, including memory and concentration disorders. When we are moving, our brain produces all kinds of natural addictive substances, such as endorphin (our natural antidepressant) and serotonin. Both substances reduce feelings of melancholy. A short walk (especially after lunch) also provides our blood with extra oxygen, which promotes the intake of glucose, thus supplying our brains with more energy. It also speeds up the removal of waste products from the body. A light lunch and a brief stroll set us up for processing new information with renewed vigor.

Furthermore, a walk is important for another reason. When you have a problem, a walk will make you literally forget your work for a while. Your brain has extra energy, the subconscious gets to work and once back at your desk the solution appears almost as if by magic. Of course, you do not always have to walk. Doing a few brief physical exercises during a break in a meeting will do the trick just as well.

Games are a lot more than a pleasant way to pass the time. They train your brain. View them as fitness exercises for the mind—as mental push-ups. Many games have different levels of difficulty and fit in with our need for achievable challenges. Because of their multimedia character, videogames are even better for actively exercising our brain. When you have to process a lot of information, it is a good idea to regularly have a break. Play a game during that break. This keeps your brain active, while it is doing something totally different. When playing games, the hormone dopamine is released, and this makes us feel good.

Playing games is also a natural activity for learning tactics and strategy, skills we need when dealing with information. In most games, we constantly have to weigh the risks and possibilities. Do we play it safe or do we take up the gauntlet? We face the same decisions when using information. We need to decide whether we have sufficient information for making a decision and, if not, when we will stop collecting data. Are we taking the risk and making a decision using the available information, or are we playing it safe and collecting more information first? By all means, do play around with your answers.

CHAPTER 7

BRAIN AT WORK

A long time ago, a teacher in personal effectiveness taught me to reflect at the end of the day. In ten minutes, think about your day: what did you do; should you have done this; what could you have done better, and more of those kinds of questions. It was one of the best pieces of advice I was ever given. This chapter also incites reflection. It shows that you have to pay attention to what you are paying attention to. Furthermore, this chapter will discuss remembering and forgetting.

PAY ATTENTION

One of the most important lessons in this book is the importance of concentration. By concentrating, we are able to recall information from our memory. However, there are two limitations to focused attention: 1) it is selective, and 2) it is very limited. After all, you never know what information was retained in your memory. Concentration and selection are necessary; otherwise, mental information overload is not far away. Attention is your most valuable resource when processing information.

How do we actually decide the tasks to which we will give our attention? Several factors play a part in this. First, the brain always gives priority to voice and faces. Even though we may be totally concentrating on something, when someone calls our name they immediately attract our attention.

Second, even if we are able to concentrate well, that is nevertheless fairly subjective and limited. We are easily distracted. Our brain has trained itself to be alert to changes and react on these.

Third, our brain has good filters for selecting information, but these filters only act when the information concerns us. A major accident abroad? The most interesting news is how many compatriots were injured. Do you work for a government agency? Then you will be immediately interested in a feature on the salaries of public servants.

Fourth, anything that has our interest will always be given priority. For example, think back to the last interesting conversation you had. Most likely, you did not consciously see anybody around you because you were already pleasantly involved in talking to someone.

Attention Deficits

Never before has our brain had to deal with so many demands for attention. No wonder this day and age brings along new illnesses. Two types of illness that stem from a lack of attention are *Attention Deficit Disorder* (ADD) and *Attention Deficit Trait* (ADT).

ADD is a *neurological* disorder that can be boosted by environmental factors. Visible manifestations are restlessness, an inability to focus attention, and the sensation of continuously missing important information. The consequences are that people start to postpone things, are forgetful, do not make deadlines, have no more time left for reflection, and are unable to concentrate.

The main cause of ADT, on the other hand, lies mainly *outside the person*. The symptoms often become visible after a while. People who suffer from this disorder find it difficult to set priorities, manage their own time, and organize information. This often leads to chaotic, hurried behavior, bursts of frenzy, gruffness, and peremptory behavior.

Nevertheless, the development of new disorders such as ADD and ADT also has a positive side. Some people want to and are able to work at high stress levels. They process information in a fast way. By properly analyzing information at the very last minute, they perform extremely well. Furthermore, their ingenuity enthuses others to perform better themselves.

Attention Manager

It is sometimes said that the average manager has a maximum attention span of two minutes. After that time, their thoughts wander to other things. That is understandable; there are many things that demand their attention. For that reason, a conversation with your manager should start by giving the conclusion of your story, whether this concerns an article or a presentation. Just leave out all introductory sentences. If you are giving a presentation and really wish to get people's attention, start by describing a personal problem or a point of interest.

Managers suffer less information stress, simply because they have more control over their work. They are able to steer their work, which subordinates are often much less able to do. However, you can learn to concentrate. By planning and organizing information, you can give your brain the opportunity to develop all kinds of routines and automate processes. These come in handy when you wish to deal unconsciously with as many tasks as possible. Unconscious actions take less effort, are more efficient, and less likely to cause errors.

One of the most valuable pieces of advice I was ever given came from a senior executive and concerned the density of information. Very early on in his career, this manager was aware that if he did not act on it, he would one day have too much information. From that moment on, he selected all information on the basis of two criteria: information density and importance. By the first criterion, he meant that a source of information should specifically deliver the desired information, and not too much excess data. In other words, he did not read a daily newspaper but instead read an online, personalized newsletter; additionally, he read specialist journals instead of "general interest" magazines. The second criterion should apply to everyone, he thought: He should receive only information and matching sources that fitted with his interest and the necessity of that particular moment—and that were especially accessible by means of proven technology.

To Multitask or Not

Multitasking appears to be the new trend. However, it is only possible when the bulk of those tasks are performed unconsciously. We can, for example, breathe and drive a car at the same time. When we do need our attention to perform a task, multitasking is no longer possible. Our brain is simply not made for multitasking. It performs individual tasks sequentially, not in parallel. Every task is given between a few milliseconds to three seconds brain time. However, the manager in your head, the prefrontal cortex, has a much harder time when it needs to keep track of several tasks simultaneously. Your attention often jumps, and that means time and time again having to pick up where you left off. Multitasking demands a lot of control information and slows us down.

Another reason is the energy supply. Per minute, your brain receives a unit of blood and, hence, energy. The brain has to divide this energy over several tasks and several brain parts. When you are multitasking, there is less energy available per part.

What about that pianist? An experiment demonstrated that you could have a pianist perform two complex tasks *simultaneously*: play a new piece and repeat a text read out loud to him. The reason is that these tasks use different input channels. The pianist *saw* the piano piece in front of him and *heard* the text read out loud. We learn from this experiment that it is possible to multitask if you use different input media, because they activate different parts of your brain.

Attention Principles

You cannot create more time. But could you possibly increase your attention? This question is as yet impossible to answer. Attention, concentration, interests, more freedom of choice, and the desire to experience everything are highly personal things. The brain attempts to arm itself against this information overload. When we are dealing with specific information, our brains deliberately stop other information.

A few principles that improve our attention are:

- The principle of reciprocity plays a major part in the working environment. If you pay attention to others, you will receive attention back.
- Give feedback regarding e-mails and other communications that do not interest you.
- Identify the information on which you wish to spend time and attention. Show this to your colleagues, or if necessary, tell them which information has your attention.
- Learn the marketing principles that lie behind attention.

- Remember that people will be only too happy to make an effort to obtain good information. If information is found too easily, our attention soon lapses. Compile summaries, for example, and do not make the information entirely available until you know more about the receiver.
- Information demands not only attention but also context, insight, and experience, all of which are provided by the people receiving the information. You cannot provide that context until you know more about the receiver. Therefore, send out as little unsolicited information as possible.
- People sometimes deliberately cut themselves off from information because things are getting too much for them or because they first wish to process the information they already have. Always go by the "less is more" principle.
- When we give attention, that means we are selecting and performing an activity that we consider important. It turns out that we can devote ourselves to a single task for 15–20 minutes. Then we do something different. At that stage, the task itself does not need to be finished.
- Don't be tempted to make certain decisions too quickly. Always postpone important decisions for a little while—usually, just a few minutes will suffice.
- Make sure that your information is strongly differentiated from the surrounding information. Color, shape, sound: Everything is allowed. Occasionally, try to fit your information in with people's fundamental fears and reflexes—for example, you can predict likely disaster scenarios should your project not be approved.
- Some people are naturally good at filtering information. Check out how they have organized their sources of information and the matters to which they give their attention.
- Use as many senses as possible to communicate information successfully.

REMEMBER TO REMEMBER

We only remember 5 percent of all the information we acquire. That is certainly not much. How can we be sure to remember more—particularly information that we really need to remember?

Memories are excellent sources of information. Recall a certain photo from your youth, for example. As soon as you see the photo again, it evokes many images and emotions. However, you never remember things exactly as they were at the time. A memory is imagination; it is always colored by all the things you are presently involved in. The present determines how you see the past. The same is true when we are recording information. We record information because we think we will want to be able to recall it at a later stage. In other words, we remember to predict the future.

Some people argue that their memory is weak. Shocking world events demonstrate that it is not all that bad. Why we remember certain events better than others has everything to do with the context of an event. Our own autobiographical memory plays a major role. We link our own stages of life to important events. We also rewrite memories of the important events in our memory.

For many years, Gordon Bell[1], who works for Microsoft, has been collecting all his digital information—books, articles, movies, music, photos, presentations, telephone conversations, chat logs—in one single location. This is known as the MyLifeBits project. Every day, all his personal information is automatically stored and indexed. It is almost as if the system that he uses replaces his own real memory. The major advantage of this external memory is that he can use a search engine for seeking specific information, something that you cannot do with a real memory. Bell views this digital storage as a possibility for telling stories about everything he has experienced. Not the individual objects, but the *stories* are to him the core of his digital life. These are constructed associatively by means of a journey he undertakes through his digital life, coupled with the necessary links. His carefully maintained external memory makes him immortal, as it were.

Most people do not need to go as far as Bell. However, the following factors are important for remembering things longer and better.

Unconscious Mind

Research shows that someone who uses his unconscious brain capacity frequently is better able to process large quantities of information. As yet, the researchers do not know exactly how this happens. Emotions play a major role in the process, that much is certain.

However, the problem is that we cannot control these unconscious processes that well.

The fact that we cannot immediately retrieve things from our memory is also connected with the way we have stored these things in our memory. When we remember information, we do so because many different connections were made. This process happens virtually automatically when we include the context of an event as much as possible in our effort. Take your time to take in all the relevant information, if you wish to remember something really well—not just words, but also smells, sounds, and preferably also your own frame of mind.

When making simple, less important decisions, it is a good idea to weigh the pros and cons. However, there are indications that when you are considering important decisions, it is better to trust your unconscious feelings. Studies repeatedly reveal that the best decisions are made after sleeping on it or simply doing something different for a while. By means of unconscious thinking, our brain makes more associations, and we will sooner arrive at alternatives. Conscious thinking usually does not lead to creative, unusual, or original solutions.

Conscious Mind

Occasionally, our memories play tricks on us. The reason for this is our brains are protecting us against too many stimuli. The brain chooses what it wishes to see and hear. Many visual games are based on things that are not actually there or movements that do not exist. Remember that what you thought you knew is not always what you saw or experienced. Alan Greenspan once put it aptly: "I know you think you understand what you thought I said, but I'm not sure you realize that what you heard is not what I meant."

Your brain is not static; at every new experience it records all recalled personal information all over again. Such an experience does not even have to be a physical one: Just thinking about it already provides new information and therefore changes a memory.

Repetition

One of the memory techniques featured in this book is repetition; I cannot repeat that often enough. Just as athletes know they have to keep training their muscles, we should know that the "muscles" of our brains also demand exercise. By exercising your brain, you enable it to make new connections, bring back memories, and remember these all over again. When we train a specific muscle too much, there will be a time when training has no more effect. It does not become any stronger. It is just the same with brains. Sudoku are great puzzles, but ten puzzles a day is a little too much of a good thing. Variation is key.

As long as we discover something new when learning information, repetition is not boring. It is, however, important to leave sufficient time between repetitions. You will often know from your own experience how long this is. If you must repeat information, try to do it in somewhat different locations. Also, repeat any information that is offered in writing out loud at least once. Audile people do this almost as a matter of course.

The abovementioned Gordon Bell has discovered an interesting possibility. He constantly wears a camera around his neck that takes many photos. At the end of the day, he plays thousands of these photos at high speed in a few minutes. In this way, he relives the entire day. It turns out that he recalls people and all kinds of details many times better.

Remember the Milk

One of the most often used external devices is a writing pad or memo pad, at least for those of us born before 1985. Writing down things that we do not wish to forget serves two purposes: 1) not forgetting and 2) learning. Writing something down is an extremely good way to remember that information. Simply the act of writing leads to a very strong memory. The pen writing down the sentence, the time it takes to make a note, the paper, and the necessity of not forgetting something—all of these are signals, telling our brain to store this information safely. It is therefore a good idea to carry paper and a pen at all times, or to make sure that you know how to record a memo in your cell phone.

Another often-used memory strategy is a short list with action items, better known as a "to-do" list, to organize and remember information. This way, we add to our memory and are able to keep our affairs in order. As soon as the tasks on your list have been completed, you throw it out. That gives you a feeling of satisfaction. In your information profile (Chapter 5) you will record which lists you use for keeping up with your activities. Especially for managers, this also has to include the lists of their supporting employees. Each list clearly states who registers things in the list, who maintains it, and where the *original* list is kept.

David Allen[2] takes things a step further. He proposes to perform a regular core dump of your brain. That results in a gigantic list of outstanding items. The advantage is that your brain is really empty at that particular moment.

Next, some practical tips regarding to-do lists:

- *Use one single system.* You can record things in several different ways, but make sure to make one of the systems the leading one.
- *Always determine the purpose of your list.* Each list should have a single purpose.
- *Develop your own code and abbreviations.* Remember that you are the only person to read this.
- *Go through the list every day.* Review items, cross them out, or change their priority.
- *If you are used to doing so, use colors, lines, and other markings.*
- *Use IT tools for changing your work.* If you are used to keeping a to-do list on paper, you should perhaps consider the electronic version. It can be handy for signaling and for links to the rest of your digital workplace.

In conclusion, two important tips: 1) do not make the list too long, and 2) also make a "not-to-do" list. That list will help you to say "no" to activities that others think you should do.

Tip of the Tongue

It is important to pay a lot of attention to other people because they are very good sources of information. Each human being is unique, and each personal contact as well. That is why people appreciate it when you know who they are, especially if you also remember a few details regarding your last encounters. So why then do you forget someone's name? Simple: The brain stores names in the left half, where language is housed. The visual part is recorded in the right half. Furthermore, we have to combine a number of recollections from different memories. We will have to remember a person in specific situations (a task of the episodic memory) and we have to know who is part of which organization (a task of the semantic memory).

There are all sorts of techniques available for better remembering people's names:

- *Take notice of the other person.* Pay attention to physical characteristics and link these to name and face. Also link these to a few details of the contact (e.g., met during a vacation in Peru, seen at a conference, spoken to at a friend's house).
- *When you meet someone, always call them by their name a few times during the meeting.* The other person will correct you in case you do not pronounce their name properly or if you did not get the right name.
- *Try to imagine the person you saw several times in the days following a meeting.* Try to remember as much as possible about this person. Possibly use the Internet to find out more about this person or add him or her to one of your social networks.
- *Make sure that the other person knows who you are.* Articulate your name. Make sure that others notice you during a meeting, and try to get them to talk about you.
- *Try to develop a knack for recalling names.* When you are convinced of its uses, it will take less of an effort.
- *Use a good strategy for filing and remembering contact details*, such as calling cards, address details at the bottom of e-mails, and printed media. Just ask if you can take a photo.
- *Do not try to remember the name of everyone you meet*; only remember those who are of interest to your network.

Recall

Ideas arrive at the most peculiar moments: in the shower, in the car, or very early in the morning. How do we remember these ideas? We can do this in a very practical way. Strategies such as sticky notes, memo recorders, or sending yourself an e-mail may help you remember things. And don't forget, your cell phone has quite a bit of storage space.

We use all kinds of memory strategies to improve our information recall. The purpose of mnemonic techniques is to improve your ability to remember difficult information and retrieve related information. The acronym HOMES, for example, can be used to help people remember the names of all the Great Lakes (Huron, Ontario, Michigan, Erie, and Superior). By means of mnemonic techniques, we better arrange and structure information. The most beautiful aspect of the method is that everybody can think them up for themselves. Be creative and invent a different mnemonic, preferably as different, colorful, or personal as possible. You are guaranteed to never forget it again.

Some students have trouble retrieving the material during an exam. The location where they acquired the information strongly differs from the location where they have to reproduce the information. By taking their mind back to the place where they studied, or by arranging their material exactly the same as they are used to doing at home, they are able to remember more.

REMEMBER TO FORGET

If we are able to remember information better, we should also be able to forget better. Some people would love to have a delete button for all those things they would rather no longer remember. Of course, there is no such button in our brain—and for good reason. Our brain does not store everything, but selects and filters only important information, certainly when this is linked to intense feelings such as fear. If we had a delete button, we might possibly delete experiences that are necessary for our survival.

Many people, often youngsters, put a lot of personal information on the Internet. Sometimes this information is even part of the collective memory. Increasingly more often, companies are seeking online information on their job applicants. Unfortunately, that information is not always correct. Therefore, you should always carefully consider what you would like others to see about you. Even if you are totally oblivious of any harm, remember that a photo is taken in a second and manipulated just as easily. The Internet does not have a delete button, either.

Many IT resources do include an option for permanently deleting information. If you share photos via Flickr or files via drop.io, you can indicate a point in time in the future at which the data will be permanently removed. Mayer-Schönberger[3] proposes to set an expiry date on each and every digital document, photograph, message, and so forth that we create.

I Forgot about That

It is very difficult to actively forget information. The more we think of something, the more connections are made. After all, that is what our brain is good at. It also explains why we are that lousy at keeping secrets. We often think about information that is known only to us. Still, here is some advice for improving your ability to forget:

- *Use conversation therapy.* When you discuss negative events with others, the chemistry in your brain changes. This happens because during such a conversation, we are linking bad experiences to a good atmosphere. This makes the bad experience less awful.
- *Create a folder on the computer, in your mail, and in your cabinet.* That folder is called: "Important information I will soon forget." What has to go in must be clear. In other words, never look in that folder!
- *Consistently ignore information sources.* This is one of the best ways to forget information. The sources could be anything: Web sites, e-mail messages, or even people.
- *Do not do everything you would do to remember better* (repetition, add context, sleep well, use more senses).
- *Do not read anything that does not interest you.* You do not need to remember it, and you also do not need to actively forget.
- *Be very busy and do as many things as possible at the same time.* You are guaranteed to forget to do a few things. Yes, these will of course also include a few truly important items. So what?
- *Do not use any to-do lists, reminders, or other physical mnemonics.* Forget to use them for real.

However, truly forgetting is only possible by *not* thinking of it. Don't you forget that!

STOP!

One of the best ways to avoid having to remember too much information or even to forget information is to stop in time. Stop looking for or asking for more information. You yourself must decide when you need to stop. It is impossible to give any clues for this. Learn from others who are able to stop in time. Some ideas on how to stop:

- If you are seeking information, then consider in advance what would constitute the best information for you as well as when you will have enough information.
- Time is an important stop criterion, rather than the agreed deadline. We are wizards at moving deadlines. Therefore, aim to stop looking for information once three-quarters of the available time is up.
- When you become frustrated because you are not finding the information, stop immediately and work out what is causing this. Are you looking at the wrong source of information? Do you have too little time? Is it unclear exactly what you are looking for? Learn from this for the next time.
- Express your search time for information in money. Or the other way around. When you stop sooner, you have earned some money or did not spend any. Allow others who ask you for information to decide whether your search time is worth its money.
- Try to find information as quickly as possible. If someone else can find it sooner than you, have that person do it for you. Smarter stopping is also smarter delegating. You may think that you have to find information yourself, but nobody is forbidding you to ask for assistance.
- Do not wait for comprehensive information. Some managers tend to first neatly arrange all acquired information and then send employees out to find any missing information. Next, they

wait until all the information is complete. This clearly is the wrong type of information behavior; certainly, it does not suit managers, whose main task is to make decisions under uncertain circumstances and based on incomplete information.

- Immediately stop when you lose interest in the information or become bored. In any case, take a mental break of at least a day or longer if possible.
- Immediately stop if you feel an aversion to going through all this newly discovered information. Ask yourself whether your information request was the right one.
- Stop earlier in the search for yet more information. There will always be some degree of uncertainty. Use your creativity to add any missing details.
- Immediately stop when you receive too much information. You have not understood the request for information correctly, or you have made the wrong selection. In the first case, you go back to the person who asked the question; in the second case, you find expert help for finding better, goal-oriented information.
- Stop when you have the slightest inkling that the answer is in the already-found information.

Remember that stopping sooner sometimes means that you do not even have to go looking. Learn to say to everyone around you: "Thanks. I have received sufficient information." Then get to work with what you were given. You reflect on it, weigh it, and then, only if you really have to, search for further information. Use the power of the unconscious part of your brain. Do not hesitate to sleep on it, look at the information problem from several perspectives, and, by all means, take your time.

Finally, another important piece of advice. When you decide to stop earlier, and from then on have your information behavior adjusted accordingly, then you should also change mentally. If you are a manager, you do not always have to be the first one to be in the know. Admit that to yourself. Rely on the people around you. They are the real information specialists in their own fields.

NOTES

1. Bell, G. & Gemmell, J. (2009). *Total recall: How the e-memory revolution will change everything.* New York: Dutton Adult.
2. Allen, D. (2008). *Making it all work: Winning at the game of work and the business of life.* New York: Viking Adult.
3. Mayer–Schönberger, V. (2009). *Delete: The virtue of forgetting in the digital age.* Princeton, NJ: Princeton University Press.

CHAPTER 8

THE INFORMATION BRAIN

Our brain helps us really forget information. It is a defense mechanism, but sometimes a nuisance when you try to find something you once remembered. It does help to simply allow less information into your brain. Select the subjects in which you are interested and wish to be an expert. This chapter teaches you which information to allow in your brain, how to better select in advance, and how to remove afterward.

SEARCH AND FIND

We often say: "If only we knew what we know already!" It would be really handy to be able to access that information depot. Our brain has developed its own ways to retrieve data. Our brain's search function is many times more powerful than any Internet search engine. Often, you can answer someone's question in a split second—if you know the answer.

We do not know exactly yet how the brain stores and retrieves information. That is why I use the metaphor of a search engine until a better comparison is found. The search engine of our brain is programmed to search in compliance with our preferences, beliefs, and the

121

context in which we live. Over time, however, that context changes. As opposed to search engines such as Google and Bing, our brain takes into account that we mainly have attention for things that touch us personally. In a city, an architect will usually see the buildings, a student the number of bars, and a hairdresser exclusive hairstyles.

Our memory has two different ways of finding information (*recognize*) and retrieving information (*recall*). A lot of information goes missing as time goes by and cannot be recalled anymore. When we are interrupted while searching for this information, we will have trouble picking up where we were. We can find things only if we know what we are looking for. Many computer users no longer organize their personal computer but use search software for their desktop. To find any of their stored information, they need the exact details of the sought information. Unfortunately, we are not that good at remembering details. We use different types of memory, such as the autobiographical and procedural memory, for storing information or references to it. In time, there is a risk of decline. We won't even remember the search terms that might conjure up the electronic information.

Never Stop Asking

To find the right information, it is important to ask the right questions of the right people. That seems obvious, but it is not. We all know people who are always asking questions. They have learned that many things become clearer by asking questions, to themselves but also to others. Other people never ask any questions. They could save themselves time and effort by allowing others to assist them in their search for information.

By asking a question, you show you are looking for information. Managers are sometimes inclined to delegate the search for information to subordinates. When they do so, they miss the opportunity to formulate the question more precisely through consultation. After all, they do not know for sure whether the employees used the right information sources to get answers to certain questions. Many managers do not give this any thought.

The trouble is that we often do not know what question to ask to get good information. The context, for example, is not fully known. Seeking and finding good information means asking smart questions first.

In a few brief sentences, you soon know which information the other person seeks and whether you are the right person for answering the question.

In my opinion, this strategy isn't used often enough. A manager asks an employee a question, preferably during meetings or via e-mail. The employee sets to work and does his or her utmost, but the result is always different from expectation. Before the actual search for information, there should always be a good dialogue. For this reason, most theories of information behavior (Chapter 4) start with a phase of discovering the real information needs. One advantage of this approach is that the information seeker does not become frustrated later in the search process when they cannot find any information or the right information.

The average employee spends more than 40 percent of his or her time on searching for information. Over 80 percent of all sought information is unstructured, impossible to express in hard figures. Once we find the information we sought, a different problem occurs: What is the quality of this information? On the Internet, there is certainly a lot of low-quality information. Often we do not know the quality. The people who are presenting this information may appear reliable, even if they are not. As a result, we may lose a lot of time in verifying the information we have found.

The Needle in the Haystack

Apart from asking good questions, other things matter when looking for information:

- Properly index your own information collections, preferably automatically. A regular pruning of your collections is no luxury. You see what you once saved and thus exercise your memory. You usually know which information you needed then but no longer need now, which makes it easy to throw things out.
- Acquaintances may help you find information, but a company has other experts available: secretaries, communication experts, librarians, or simply the smartest person in your department.
- You can only find information that was once indexed and is accessible if you know and use the right search concepts. Therefore, check whether your desktop search engine is properly installed.

- Because searching with a search engine is so easy, hardly anybody asks actively for help when searching for good quality information. Therefore, the ease of a search engine is at the same time its major disadvantage. Each search term delivers many results. But does that information answer your question?
- The effect of role models is generally known. A famous person such as Oprah Winfrey can be a powerful motivator, for example, for people who wish to lose weight. It is just the same with information. If people whom you consider important say that you should handle information better, there is a large chance that you will do so.
- Sometimes we don't know the right people or we don't know how to get to the information that will make our lives much easier. We are not even informed of what we need to know. But you also need to know what you don't want to know. Your information profile also includes areas that don't interest you.
- Be critical of information that shows you the opposite of what you expect. You may think it is better to completely ignore that information, and that nobody will ever find out. However, the strength of a good information worker is to collect all information and evaluate it correctly.
- People are lazy by nature. As soon as they think they know what the other person wishes to hear, they stop searching for information. A lot of information is ignored because it does not fit in with their frame of reference or simply does not fit their knowledge area.

SAVE EVERYTHING

Once they have found it, people have to decide what to do with this information. For a lot of information this is immediately obvious: It is useless to them. Or just of temporary importance, such as, for example, the exact parking space near that mall. Part of the information is important for the task or activity of that particular moment. Yet a lot of information remains that requires a decision: saving or discarding. Saving too much information will present problems later on at retrieval and therefore takes time and effort. Saving too little information can also be a problem. You lack knowledge and that may cost money.

Why do we save information? Jones[1] provides four reasons:

1. *The information is irreplaceable.* Some information is unique, once-only, and irreplaceable: for example, your high school diploma, photos of loved ones, and love letters.
2. *The information is hard to replace.* This includes documents like identity cards, tax data, and car papers. Much of this data is rarely needed, but it is better to keep it yourself. Otherwise, should you ever need it, retrieving will take extra time and effort.
3. *The information is part of a collection.* The owners of collections tend to pursue completeness. Music, recipes, pictures of their idols—they want to have all. This is not about the individual information object, but about the collection.
4. *Work information.* This information regarding what we are actually doing, such as project tasks, phone numbers, and current documents.

You can use this breakdown for checking whether you should keep information. If the information is unique or hard to replace, then keep it in a safe place.

However, people also use other strategies for saving information. First, you can simply ignore information. If you don't see the information, you don't have to decide whether to save it or not. Sometimes this approach is not a bad choice, especially when you are surrounded by colleagues who file absolutely everything. Second, you can decide to simply file everything. After all, the desktop search engine will index everything. The third strategy is to collect everything and process it later. Going through all your documents or electronic files once a week is not a bad idea either. Fourth, you can of course set filters. This will vastly reduce the number of decisions to be made. Virtually all IT systems have such a facility. Admittedly, the theory of "accidental information" no longer applies, because you will miss that type of information. The last strategy for not having to save anything is simply to receive as little as possible. Just make your decisions under high levels of uncertainty.

There is a lot of hard work going on in developing techniques that help us recognize the information we previously saved. By visualizing recorded information, you will more quickly know what you already know. You may recognize this situation: Have you ever been browsing through your e-mail history or reading the folders on your computer and come across documents that you forgot you had?

ORDER, PLEASE

Until recently, human beings stored information in their brains and passed it on to others in the best oral tradition. These days, people have to store information elsewhere, because their memory is no longer capable of handling all the information presented to it. Today's people have to use some kind of classification mechanism. Everyday life gives numerous examples of why categorization of information often leads to frustration, problems, or even worse. Anyone who has ever been shopping in the local supermarket knows how difficult it sometimes is to find what you want. If you are looking for apples, you go the fruit and vegetable department. But apple juice is stored on a shelf in another part of the store altogether, as are applesauce or apple pie filling. Some stores have rearranged their products to fit together logically for the time these are to be consumed: You can find everything you need for a good dinner in one location.

When we were young, the world seemed very orderly. Holiday pictures were printed on special paper and stuck in an album or kept in an old shoebox. Besides, we did not have thousands of photos then. So it was easy to find them and when we looked at them again, we remembered all the events they pictured.

It was no different with early electronic documents. A document name could be only eight characters, which led to creative, often incomprehensible abbreviations. We had to regularly clean up and reorganize our computers. Lack of space and inherent tidiness determined how and when we saved and organized our information. Furthermore, we had ample time to deal with this organization. Every time we organize physical media or digital files differently, we learn anew what we consider important.

As Weinberger[2] notes, we are used to first-order organization, sorting and arrangement of the objects themselves, as well as to second-order organization, information about information (metadata), which is sorted in a different way. However, in the digital world, a third order of organization is emerging that is undoing many of our old assumptions. No physical object can be in two places at once. But in the electronic world, we can file each object over and over again, in various locations and in various versions. Furthermore, as Weinberger contends, the owners of information (such as companies) no longer own the organization of that information. Users can sort and organize information in any way that suits their needs.

Brain Order

Everyone wants to understand the world around us. Fortunately human beings, in particular our brains, have a cognitive capacity that comes in very handy. We view our environment from two perspectives.

The first perspective examines the *differences* within the material. The other perspective is based on the *similarities* of the various objects. Someone who arranges often focuses on one of the two perspectives. You can arrange your bedding by bed; you can also arrange by sheets, pillowcases, color, or season. There is no right or wrong perspective, just different.

Our brain mainly uses grouping for organizing the avalanche of information. We are excellent "groupers"—unfortunately so, as we often take grouping too far. Everything must fit in a category: black-white, man-woman, Generation X-Y-Baby. Our brain also automatically emphasizes the differences between the groups and minimizes the differences within the group. In fact, dividing a group of people at random automatically leads to an almost innate rivalry between the groups.

We do this kind of classifying all day long, often without being aware of it. Also remember that grouping occurs in people all over the world. However, we are as yet not certain whether this brain capacity is inborn, just like our linguistic aptitude. Therefore, be aware that very often you will place new things or new people in a category automatically, especially when these things or people fit in a category that feels good to you. For once, postpone your judgment. Check whether the classification criterion is the right one. Surprise your brain with a new perspective.

The New Order

Next, a recommendation: Check whether your personal way of arranging is the right one. Explain to a random person in less than 30 seconds why you chose that classification. If you succeed, you have the right classification. You have to be able to provide a brief explanation for all possible storage systems: the organization of your e-mail folders, cabinets, digital photos, and financial administration, for example. If you are unable to do this, then ask the other person to help you organize your information collections better. Another person will have an entirely different view on your collection.

You can group information according to five principles: 1) location, 2) alphabet, 3) time, 4) category, and 5) hierarchy.[3] Often, these principles are combined. There is not a single good way of arranging, but you will make things easy on yourself and others when you are consistent within a classification or subclassification. Therefore, make sure to arrange the different levels of a classification logically. Because we mostly work in teams, it is even more important to use a good arrangement system.

There are several ways to arrange your information archives:

- Use just one single system per collection of objects.
- Be sure to have a maximum of ten subdivisions per division. You cannot keep track of more. (Arranging in alphabetical order is the exception to this rule.)
- Once you have identified the structure of your information organization, ask some of your close colleagues or friends for independent advice. They will often provide a fresh outlook and can help you avoid obvious pitfalls.
- At least twice a year, each archive requires maintenance. This goes for both physical as well as electronic archives. Throw things out, reorganize, and if necessary, inform others of the new organization of your archives. By the way, having no system is also a system.

- Be led by your own preferences. Allow external advice, but choose what you prefer.
- Use as many tags (information labels in the shape of key words) as possible for your electronic archives. Ask your IT coach for help if you aren't familiar with tags.
- Remember to regularly check whether the chosen arrangement is still workable. In business environments, this part of the process is typically forgotten. Joint electronic spaces require maintenance, especially because people with many different information habits record all their data in these.
- When working in teams, make one single person responsible for the setup and maintenance of joint information sources. Allow the rest of the team to occasionally give feedback on optimizing the process.
- Arranging and pruning on a regular basis is in itself a fun activity. You come across information that you forgot you had. Furthermore, you are actively using your brain during this activity to reintroduce some order. It's mental fitness in a way.
- As a guru once said: "Information is like an oyster: It has its greatest value when fresh." If you know in advance that information is obsolete or of no further use after a specific date, then mark that date. There are already a number of tools that can help automatically delete redundant information.

FILTER

Modern communication and IT resources always aim at the average user, even though there is no such person. However, many people do not adjust the standard setting of programs such as Outlook. It would, however, save a lot of time and frustrations if we were to take the trouble of setting some smart filters for the programs that we use. After all, in conversations with others, we do filter.

When visiting a city for the first time, you book a tour with an experienced guide. That guide is in fact the filter of a group of tourists. He or she knows the purpose of our visit to the city and what we wish to see. A guide may also adjust the program to satisfy specific customers. In business situations, employees are often given much information that they do not need for their job. As a tourist, they would have said something about that early in the tour.

Filters are aimed at stopping unimportant information, not for letting through important information. You can set filters for your e-mail, portal, news feeds, and so on. This way, you know that the information that gets through is interesting and important to you. Company executives often have secretaries who stop unimportant information and people and only let through what is important to the executive.

How *you* should set filters is a different story. If you don't know, then ask someone, read the manual, or just try. Filters select information on the basis of criteria that you select, and thus control your thinking process. Many people are afraid that they might miss important information when they set filters. It will usually not come to that. Other people will draw your attention to information, should you miss it. It is nevertheless important to regularly adjust your filters to your constantly changing information requirements.

An important remark has to be made. When other people act as your filters, it is sometimes hard to find out whether and why they share or don't share certain information with you. With electronic filters you know what you get, but you often cannot find out which information was stopped. Furthermore, in many electronic filters it is not always clear what the filter or selection criteria are. Sometimes accidental information is also very important. Therefore, weigh carefully between being well-informed and receiving interesting but sometimes superfluous information when setting filters.

A few tips for better filtering information:

- Always select. Determine the information areas in which you wish to be really good.
- Filter all information. (Not filtering can also be a way of filtering.)
- Tell others that you filter information, how you do so, and on which basis.
- Regularly check whether your information sources are still up-to-date. Change the criteria, if necessary.
- Find out what other people's filters (i.e., interest and preferences) are. Tailor your messages to these.

- Use as many filtering techniques as possible. Make it easy for yourself. You really remember less filter criteria than you think.
- If you do not use the acquired information, amend the filters of the information source in question. That could also involve people, whom you inform that you are not interested (anymore).

INFORMATION PRUNING

Humans are very curious by nature. Children are often more curious than adults. They never stop asking questions. This way they learn a lot about what they can and can't do. Originally, this was a survival mechanism. These days, curiosity is mainly a search for yet more information. After all, we need information to survive. Everyone who aspires to be an expert in a certain field has a strong urge to find out everything about it.

Inquisitive people often have great difficulty in pruning incoming information. Everything is of interest to them and they never get enough. However, our brain lives according to the maxim "Use it or lose it." Information that isn't used for a long time is removed. And as time goes by, an increasing number of connections in our brain disappears. Scientists agree that this "pruning" is characteristic to a mature brain. Pruning is needed for growing up. We gain more experience when we throw out any surplus on a regular basis. At the same time, the existing connections become stronger.

Just as the connections in our brain cells need a regular pruning, we also need to regularly prune our information sources. Wouldn't it be nice if the sources that we do not use periodically would automatically disappear? A magazine we no longer read will take itself automatically to the wastebasket. Digital newsletters we immediately delete would no longer arrive in our mailbox. Unfortunately, this does not happen by itself; we have to actively cancel this information. Do this, for example, once every quarter. Take this opportunity to adjust your information profile as well.

It is easy to recognize that you have to prune. You will see, for instance, that within your team, a lot of time and money are wasted because many people collect the same information. Your colleagues cannot find information (anymore) because it is stored all over the place.

Decision-making is also delayed because people are waiting for reliable information.

However, you can also recognize the signs in yourself. You may notice, for example, that the sheer amount of information stops you from properly selecting and appreciating the right information. You do search, but often find nothing or the not the right information. This means you, too, waste time and money.

Questions to Ask

Before you start pruning, you need to know what you want to know. In your information profile (Chapter 5), your fields of interest are listed. How do you find out which fields of information have your interest? Ask yourself the following questions:

- What do you want to be or become good at doing? It is better to know a lot about a little than (too) little about a lot. Ask yourself what the added value would be to you personally if you knew a lot about a particular subject. Would it make you happier or provide more status?
- What do others think of your level of knowledge? In which field of information are you an expert to them? Just as you rely on others for certain information, you are also a source of information to others. Limit the number of information fields in which you wish to be expert. Dare to be honest about this to others.
- Do you need information from a specific knowledge area for current or future decisions?
- Is someone else already expert in this field? Then you don't need to be the expert. Good managers know what knowledge their employees have.
- Is data on a certain subject easily retrieved? Then you really don't need to remember that information.

Next, examine your information environment. Use one or more of your areas of expertise and ask yourself the following six questions:

1. *Source*. Where does my information come from?
2. *Frequency*. How often do I get this information?

3. *Time.* How much time does it take me to seek this information?

4. *Value.* Does the information hold value to me? Does this information help me achieve my goal?

5. *Need.* Does this information help me, or can I live and work without it?

6. *Working differently.* Is there a faster way to obtain this information? Do I know anyone who can do this better or faster than me?

By examining your information environment, you gain insight into whether you spend your time well, still use the right information sources, and use each source in the right manner. Superfluous information is just mental ballast and can be pruned.

Take-Outs

When you start pruning, do this at a quiet moment: Ask yourself the following questions, so you know better where to begin.

- Which information do I really need for my work?
- Which part of this information is necessary for my decisions or do I find interesting?
- Which information is useful or desirable but not necessary?
- Which information (just) stimulates my interest?
- What information do I wish to be able to talk about and do I collect only for that reason?
- Which information can I afford to lose without getting burned?
- What changes in my life if I lack certain information?

If you really cannot or don't want to prune yourself, then ask for help. Talk to a real "gardener," or in other words, an information coach. No doubt he or she knows a few handy pruning techniques. Everyone occasionally needs some guidance to learn ways to better handle information.

These days, some managers choose to give their own interpretation of the principle of being "well-informed." They select a good quality newspaper and one or two renowned journals. They read these carefully.

They assume that if something is truly important, those media will give this some attention at a given time. Not a bad method, and entirely in line with my pruning advice.

NOTES

1. Jones, W. (2008). *Keeping found things found: The study and practice of personal information management.* Amsterdam: Morgan Kaufmann.
2. Weinberger, D. (2007). *Everything is miscellaneous: The power of the new digital disorder.* New York: Times Books.
3. Wurman, R. S. (1989). *Information anxiety.* New York: Bantam Doubleday Dell Publishing Group.

CHAPTER 9

INFORMATION AT WORK

Many a software company cheerfully announces that their latest technology provides the solution to all information issues. But technology alone does not provide good information. People are needed for that. Technology is just the packaging. Technology can never provide the rich content and context that people can add to data.

Also, we should not forget that for many people, technology is not a goal in and of itself. Consider plumbing: Pipes, sink drains, valves, fixtures, and other materials are used to carry water, but the user at the receiving end only thinks, "Is the water clean and fresh?" or "Do I need this kind of water?" or "I'm thirsty!"

It is time to focus on the *I* rather than the *T* in the world of information technology.

LEARN SMARTER

Young people today ask: Why do we have to learn so much when it is so easy to find everything on the Internet? Why would you record personal information yourself? After all, information is available all the time and everywhere!

It is impossible to phrase a simple answer to these questions. It is clear, however, that you don't have to store masses of information in your brain. And our brains forget a lot. Therefore, you have to know *what* you want to know. Which information will make a difference to you and yours? You need to nurture significant information and knowledge. You made an effort to remember it and attached value to it, otherwise you would never have stored the information this well. Intelligent people know they don't have to know everything. Only two things are important to you: What do you know (and especially, what don't you know)? And what does someone else know (better)?

Better learning means learning to learn. It means learning why we remember certain information well and simply forget other information. As yet, most people are not trained in this. We have to teach ourselves and our children how to deal better with future, often unknown, situations involving much new information.

Our brain is predominantly interested in general rules rather than hard facts, because general rules take less storage space and can be used for many more things. They include less specific information. The details that the brain remembers mainly apply to life-threatening or otherwise fearful or stressful situations. We do not learn general rules by heart, but distill them from examples and situations. Our education should focus more on acquiring general rules instead of facts and data we can easily look up.

Learning smarter can also be seen from someone else's perspective. When you teach someone, you need to assess that person's level of general knowledge, their learning style, and what they already know about the subject. For that reason, you ask repeatedly for feedback and analyze their reaction to your words and behavior. Learning smarter starts with knowing how to inspire and motivate yourself and others.

In school, I was taught the power of repetition. It is best to approach a text we have to learn in several different ways: read out loud, make a summary, tell someone else. By using repetition and variation, we allow our brain to make new connections each time. "The more links and associations, the higher in the list of results," the founders of Google would say.

To be able to learn a lot, your linguistic competence needs to be well developed. After all, language is often the vehicle of our thinking. However, we also learn by means of three-dimensional representations. Both techniques are important for processing information.

Information Literacy Skills

The present information society appeals to our cognitive skills. More and more, people have to process a great deal of information to make often complex decisions. It seems to be taken for granted that we know how to deal with this information effectively. We teach our children technical skills and develop their personal competencies, but their information skills still do not receive sufficient attention.

Information literacy is a talent and set of abilities that enables individuals to recognize when information is needed. To be information literate is to be capable of locating, evaluating, and effectively using needed information. Information literacy skills help people develop lifelong learning habits.

Information literacy skills taught in an educational environment might not have the same relevance in workplace practice. The formal school information environment is linear and systematic; the information environment at work is complex, messy, and often difficult for the individual to navigate and mentally map. The information-literate employee is a critical thinker and problem solver. He or she has the ability to employ generic information activities as scaffolding to build and construct information pathways in problem-solving, decision-making, and, most importantly, the creation of new knowledge.[1] And as with children, people need "time to play" with what they learn. Many employees today are so busy in their jobs that they don't do anything that isn't immediately relevant to the tasks at hand.

These days, very few boardrooms have information literacy on the agenda. There are indicators that information literacy is being recognized at some levels as an important enabler of information workers, but this has not yet translated into widespread adoption of information literacy as a core competency within the organization. One reason is that many senior managers, the decision-makers of most companies, were educated when information usage in organizations was still in its infancy. Attaining information literacy means understanding that information is a valuable competitive resource and should be managed and used as such.

Managers must be not only information literate but also knowledgeable about information and the extent to which it can be ambiguous, contradictory, and unreliable. Furthermore, information sharing all depends on the mind-set and personal example of managers. If they do not practice the right information behavior, their employees will not have sufficient trust and confidence that managers will use information correctly and behave consistently.[2]

Learning Principles

If you wish to learn something well, it is a good idea to take note of a few important learning principles:

- We remember information better when we are emotionally involved.
- We best remember information from pictures.
- Learning is remembering what you are interested in.
- We learn skills more quickly when they are used in our everyday lives.
- We are better at remembering information that has our interest and attention.
- Unexpected or peculiar information with its immediate context is stored better.
- It is better to exercise our brain in short, intensive periods (e.g., a quarter of an hour) with short breaks in between. Do something entirely different during that break, such as a physical activity.
- Repeat the subject matter to be learned over varying periods, each time using a slightly different approach. For instance, first read sentences in a foreign language, then listen to a radio broadcast or podcast in the language, and then talk with another person in that language.
- Eating well and sufficient fresh air are vital.
- Use as many senses as possible to store information powerfully.
- Never learn in order to do someone a favor or because others think that you should know something.

Information Processing

Next, a few practical rules that will help you reduce the time you spend processing information:

- *Delegate more.* Shift some information work to others who work at a lower hourly rate than yours. Provided with good instructions, they may achieve a lot, especially when they are very organized and have a less stressful job. Do tell others that you are still there for them.
- *Allow fewer disturbances.* The longer the period you can work uninterrupted on a single job, the better. Ideally, you should spend up to 15 to 20 minutes continuously on a single activity.
- *Take more risk.* Take risks more often, instead of finding more information before making decisions.
- *Have fewer meetings.* Hold meetings less frequently, and make the meetings shorter. Use new technology such as videoconferencing and collaboration software for these meetings.
- *Organize your workplace well.* Make sure to have a workplace that is ergonomically sound and is a pleasant space to work.
- *Use collective intelligence.* There are many self-help books with tips and tricks. Set yourself the task of carrying out a minimum of ten tips from such a book.
- *Organize on Saturday morning.* Use the start of the weekend for organizing your information tasks and rearranging your priorities.

Finally, my best advice. We all struggle with the question: "What should we really know for our work?" The answer is easily found by asking yourself two questions:

1. *Which information do I owe to whom?* Talking will help you find out who expects which information from you.
2. *What do I need to enable me to give this due information?* You find out which information you need when and in what shape.

When you consistently ask these two questions, you reduce the amount of communication that takes place but you also make it more effective. Many people provide information that others never requested, or they provide too much information, provide information at the wrong moment, or provide information they know does not fit in with the recipient's level.

INFORMATION PRODUCTIVITY

In the last 50 years, computers have become much faster in processing information. Unfortunately, we ourselves have not started to speak or listen more quickly. We have invented all kinds of technological tools for making our lives more enjoyable, but to date, no gadget has been developed that helps our brain process large quantities of information. A lot of research is still needed to determine how we can measure and increase our information productivity.

Managers have four ways to increase their information productivity:

1. *Ignore.* Stop searching for information sooner. When you receive information, focus your attention on the main part of it.
2. *Filter.* Develop and use technical filters that select information on the basis of your information profile.
3. *Decide.* Allow people to take responsibility for their own tasks; when necessary, check afterward.
4. *Learn.* Make sure that people who are allowed to make decisions are actually able to do so. Train them and inform them on the conditions and the effects of their information decisions.

Finally, a consideration regarding the use of information. In the past, you borrowed a book from someone and when you gave it back, you told that person what you thought of the book. Today, we link all information to each other via the Internet. Using search engines and based on syntax, semantics, and reputation, we can find out where our information goes. However, as yet, the Web is one-way. We publish and consume, but we don't know what others do with our information.

For example, consider a magazine article that is made available on the Web in PDF format. We can see who reads it, copies it, and prints it, but it is not recorded in the document what anyone does with all or part of the contents. Now that would be a real revolution: recording social context within an information object, enabling us to see who does what with our information.

Addicted to Information

The brain plays an important role in information overload. The *nucleus accumbens* or motivation center is a small area in the brain that plays a part in addictions. If there is more activity in this area, then dopamine production increases. Dopamine makes us feel good. That feeling can be induced by addictives such as coffee, alcohol, or amphetamine but also by motivation factors such as the desire for money. When we win, the dopamine level in our motivation center rises.

However, our brain does not distinguish between normal motivation factors such as money or status and addictives such as alcohol or drugs. When people are addicted to drugs, the motivation center will reduce its own production of dopamine because the stimuli of addictives are many times stronger than, for example, the desire for money. This is how an addict gets trapped in a vicious circle. The motivation center is taken over by the addictives and cannot focus on anything else. That explains why it is so difficult to kick the habit.

Managers can become addicted to power and success. After all, these increase their dopamine production. It can even become difficult for them to give up their high positions voluntarily. Receiving attention is also addictive; that is one of the reasons the Rolling Stones are still performing. And it has been scientifically proven: You can become addicted to the latest gadgets, just as you can become addicted to getting a head start or having better or more information than someone else.

Information Value

In Chapter 1, I stated that the value of information is difficult to determine. A simple word like "No" may have serious financial and emotional consequences (consider, for example, if it is your answer to the county clerk on your wedding day!).

The feeling that we receive too much information is partially caused by having to value information all through the day. Previously, we had a limited number of information sources: the media, our boss, our own network. We knew quite accurately how reliable these sources were. Today, we have many virtual friends, we are able to find huge amounts of information using search engines, and our mailboxes fill up with all sorts of messages. For each piece of information we receive, we have to ascertain whether it is useful and valuable to us.

Recent research shows that our prefrontal cortex and the production of dopamine ensure that not all incoming information gets through to our gray matter. We can switch this information shield on and off at will. Dopamine is the switch. Using this neurotransmitter, we select the right actions and are capable of remembering these. Dopamine also makes us feel good. This means that the brain is not only able to select the right information; it also rewards the body afterward. There is even research that suggests that setting goals promotes dopamine production. This could explain why some people give away their information freely, even though they endured great pain in obtaining it. Sharing their information is enough reward for these people.

We cannot appreciate some information until we have seen it or made it our own. We don't know whether a book is good until we have read it. The same goes for a restaurant or a show. Afterward, we know whether the meal or the show were worth the money. That is why we love evaluation sites. They provide subjective impressions, but many evaluations added together provide fairly objective information.

Information Culture

Information consists of data in a specific context, and this context is decided by a person. Therefore, information is particularly linked with other people. If you wish to handle information more productively, you will have to listen and pay better attention to others. What does the other, for example, know about the subject you provide information on? How willing is the other person to share their information or knowledge with you?

Whether a person is prepared to share information or not is related to the information culture within an organization or society. Such a culture is based on norms and values and influences people's opinions on exchanging information. The information culture is mainly involved with soft factors: "That is how we do things," or "We are an open organization," or "It is absolutely prohibited to spread information outside the group."

If you think the information culture within your company needs to change, then start at the top. Management has to lead by example! All workers within a company must have free access to information that is important to them.

How is the information culture in your organization doing? Answer the following questions:

- How quickly and easily do you gain access to all information you want and can have at any given time?
- Are you able to share information with anyone within and outside the organization easily?
- Can you do your job when and where you choose to? And in doing so, do you have the same information available as at your workplace?
- How easy is it to contact people who do not work in the same department but with whom you wish to share information?
- What is the answer when you ask people to share information with you?

The last question in particular is a good indication of the state of the information culture. Of course, you also need to ask yourself questions:

1. Do you have the right attitude toward the use and sharing of information?
2. Are you constantly looking for better information for your organization?
3. Does your information behavior match what your organization wants?

Information culture is also important to managers and their personal assistants. Good managers ensure that their assistants are well informed, will take care of a lot of preliminary work, know what is important, and especially know their managers' information profiles. This also includes regular consultation on how they can best communicate with each other, on learning from each other what should receive attention and which information sources are still relevant.

SMART INFORMATION WORKERS

Smart or intelligent people are very able to process information and understand what is asked of them. Intelligent people often have to make an effort to accomplish certain tasks. However, because they perform these tasks more often, their brains are better trained.

Our intelligence is controlled by several prejudices: Big is better, different is dangerous, and visible is important. It is good to be aware of these reflexes. In stress situations, we often revert to our primal intelligence without being aware of it. At one time, these reflexes were useful for our survival, but these days they are often not subtle enough.

Smart information workers know that self-knowledge is the best means for using information well. If you wish to change your information behavior, for example, you will first need to know why you do what you do and what you can do to change your habits. Your information profile (see Chapter 5) is an important tool in this. This profile describes your aptitude, attitude, and behavior regarding information.

Smart people seem to get ideas more often than others: in the shower, in the car, or very early in the morning. These locations all have characteristics that a workplace doesn't have. In the shower we feel relaxed and calm. All senses are stimulated. In the car, a similar thing happens. We mainly drive on autopilot, immersed in our thoughts. Nobody tells us what to do or what to think about. This allows us to access the unconscious part of our brain. During the night, our brain has been busy reorganizing information. It figures that new ideas appear almost automatically upon wakening.

When you do get ideas like this, make sure to record them. Writing pads, sticky notes, or a PDA are fine for this purpose. You can also use these when, during the day, through books, articles, people, or your own thoughts, you get ideas that are worth further investigation. If you don't record these, then it's likely you will forget most of your ideas by the end of the day.

You don't become a smart information worker just like that. But you can do certain things that make you handle information more astutely. Some advice:

- *Manage your own calendar.* Deliberately reserve time in your calendar for difficult tasks. Remove things you don't really like from your calendar.
- *Manage your time.* Divide your time into large chunks. The more different information tasks you have, the more sense it makes to divide this into large units.

- *Be susceptible.* Open yourself up to new information, even though it does not fit with what you currently know or think. The power of philosophers is their open attitude towards other views.
- *Be ignorant.* People think they have to be able to talk about everything. However, you really don't need to know it all. It is a relief to just admit that you don't have to and don't know everything. Acknowledging your ignorance is an ideal basis for learning new things.
- *Be aware of the information that you supply.* When providing information, always think of the recipient. Their level of knowledge, background, and situation may be different from what you expect. If you don't know the person you are giving information to, then try to find out more about him or her.
- *Do one thing at a time.* Most people cannot perform two information tasks simultaneously, particularly if these require mental effort. Only allow brief disturbances by e-mail or telephone when these don't demand too much of your thinking. Seclude yourself from intrusions.
- *Let go.* When you need to solve a difficult problem, depend more on your subconscious. Let go of the problem and do something totally different. When you think about the problem again, the solution will arrive sooner.
- *Get to know yourself.* Discover, possibly together with someone you trust, why you collect all this information. Know what drives you. Why do you collect information, organize it, and throw it away later on?
- *Develop empathy.* You are one of the lucky ones who understands why you need less information for your life and your work. Do not judge others too quickly if they don't know, do not immediately understand something, or (in your opinion) give the wrong answers. And don't judge them when they collect too much information.
- *Slow down.* Take more time to digest the information that you already have. Do not search for more information. It takes extra energy you will never earn back.

Smart information workers are people who have known the information presented in Part II of this book for a long time and apply these measures in their daily lives. They know their own information profiles, know how they handle information, and act on this.

TECHNOLOGY SMART

Information technology is to some extent responsible for the current overload of information. Yet the same technology also has capabilities that can be used for better, more personalized access to the right information, at the right time, in the right format, and with the right tools.

A large number of tools are available to help address the human bottleneck by increasing productivity. At the same time, there is a shift toward users having to install and maintain their own information services: People use ATMs, check themselves in at the airport, or use smart phones to do what they need to do. Also, intelligent, machine-based filters and automated decision-makers (e.g., intelligent agents) are steering information behavior in the right direction.

Using Tools Better

Use the following rules for each new device or new software package. Apply these rules particularly when others think you should use that new solution.

- *Select the right IT tool for your work.* Sometimes, it is useful to know why something was invented. Listen to the experts in the field—the ones who are the early adopters. They are in the best position to advise you against falling into the same traps they might have fallen into before.
- *Learn the basic skills for each IT tool.* Learn one or two new functions or tricks every day. Preferably do this via your colleagues.
- *Ask and keep asking others for tips, tricks, and ways for working smarter.* A lifehacker, for example, is someone who solves problems in a smart and nonobvious way. Lifehacks are the various techniques they use to do this.
- *Talk to someone born after 1985.* Learn how they use technologies such as blogs, wikis, Twitter, and search engines. Ask yourself how these tools might help you.

- *Use IT tools to change your work.* Have you always kept a "to-do" list on paper? Consider the electronic version. This is also useful for signaling and for links to the rest of your digital workplace.
- *For a whole year, reserve a minimum of one hour a week for getting better acquainted with the software that you use.*
- *For once, consider not buying the latest gadgets.* Alternately, postpone this purchase for a somewhat longer period. It gives peace.
- *Learn the IT tools that you have had for a while all over again.* You will see that you have learned things incorrectly, or that tasks can be performed more efficiently. For example, reread the pages on search tips for the search engine that you use.

Technology Is Helpful

Technology helps us to better consume information. All details are recorded. Our memory only records the main information. When meeting another person, we would sooner register (for example) a firm handshake than the brand of the shoes they wear. On the Internet, we can see nearly everything. But do we need to? Our brain can teach us a thing or two. It makes sure just to store and remember important information.

Receiving too many sensory stimuli can cause ADHD. Technology is both an important cause as well as a possible solution for people with ADHD. They can benefit from so-called neurofeedback. With this technique they can put themselves and their brains in the right mood. They learn in which situations they become restless, what causes of their lack of ability to concentrate, why they want to do that much at the same time, and why they never finish things.

However, technology can mean more to people. We all occasionally worry about our memory. After all, our two main fears are not leading a healthy lifestyle and memory problems in later life. Most of us know someone who suffers from the early stages of dementia or Alzheimer's.

People with Alzheimer's often become frustrated because they can remember little or nothing about the recent past. They are no longer able to link then and now. Practitioners advise these people to talk a lot to their family and friends. People with Alzheimer's can also benefit vastly from keeping a blog. By telling their story to family and friends, they are making connections with the recent past in a modern way. Of course, that does not bring back their memories, but by means of blogging they are able to shape their daily experiences themselves. A blog helps them to keep in touch with the world around them. Furthermore, fellow sufferers are often better positioned than family or friends to understand their experiences and provide them with practical advice on what to do and what not.

The main thing a blog does for people with Alzheimer's is adding a new *experience* to their memory. Getting angry because they can't remember events or people any longer serves no purpose. A blog does. A blog gives them an external memory that is always available. The only problem is that older people are not experienced in using Web 2.0 technologies. This could be a nice task for anyone wishing to devote themselves to assisting humanity. After all, in the future, wouldn't we all like someone to help us with the technologies of that time?

Digital Workplace

We are witnessing a plethora of new tools and digital services to access information. Information workers are constantly searching for relevant information and, at the same time, evaluating all of it for its usefulness for the task at hand. A first and necessary step in becoming an informed and productive information worker lies in organizing access to information from one virtual area: the digital workspace, a combination of physical equipment and integrated access to all internal and external information flows, including several easy-to-use applications for that information. The objective of such a workplace is to deliver the right information anywhere in the world to the right person and at the right time.

Check whether in your work the following matters are organized regarding your information environment. Otherwise, consult with the IT department to find out when this will be the case. These facilities are the minimum required for being able to function properly as an information worker:

- *Personalization.* Employees can set up their digital workplace entirely according to their own views. Part of the parameters are directly linked to the preferences and working methods as laid down in the information profile.
- *Filters.* Using filters and based on their profiles, employees themselves can arrange which information they do or do not receive. Where possible, workplace systems analyze current information behavior and periodically propose changes for delivering better and more specific information.
- *Integrated search facilities.* Employees can simultaneously search information in several internal and external sources. The presentation of the results fits with the employee's preferences (visual, arranged in chronological order or per project, etc.).
- *Integrated communication.* All means of communication link perfectly. The digital workplace arranges switching-on or switchover without loss of functionality.
- *Signaling.* Just like people, digital workplaces can be set up to report news according to the criteria of the user.
- *Searching for people.* The digital workplace has a function to easily find people within the organization. They can be members of social networks, virtual teams, or other organizations. This function is automatically linked to all available communication systems and to each person's information and communication profile.
- *A unique interface.* All information sources and all systems within and outside the organization can be approached via a single user-friendly interface.

Digital workplaces are becoming increasingly more an extension of us, especially of our memory. Many of the latest cell phones and similar gadgets already include functions that support your brain well. Even stronger, they are not just an extension of your hands, ears, and eyes. As far as content is concerned, they are indispensable as well. As someone said to me recently: "If I lose my cell phone, I lose part of my memory."

Some of the brain's tasks are taken over by smart devices. Such a device reminds someone that it is time for their medication, recalls the name of the person they just met, and advises them to visit someone again. There will certainly be a time when human beings can no longer function properly without the aid of these intelligent devices.

NOTES

1. Lloyd, A. (2003). Information literacy: The meta-competency of the knowledge economy? An exploratory paper. *Journal of Librarianship and Information Science, 35*(2), 87–92.
2. Marchand, D. A. (Ed.) (2000). *Competing with information: A manager's guide to creating business value with information content.* London: John Wiley & Sons.

CHAPTER 10

CLEVER COMMUNICATION

It took us millions of years to develop a good visual memory. That memory is still very important to us. After all, we remember images faster and better than we remember text. We have only had language at our disposal for around 10,000 years and are slowly coming to grips with it.

This chapter discusses ways of transferring information using stories and images, among other things. And, just like the rest of Part II, it is about making improvements to your information behavior and increasing your information processing capacity.

COMMUNICATE INFORMATION

We communicate by means of language. The brain hardly knows any other way for making something clear to other people, aside from our nonverbal body language. Although from an evolutionary point of view the ability to speak in words has not existed very long, the human brain adjusted to the new skill very quickly. A four-day-old baby already recognizes its mother's sound and voice, and toddlers learn their mother tongue super-fast.

Language is an important means of transferring information. People love to talk to each other. When conducting a conversation, we prefer to see the other person if possible. With every interaction and every word we read or hear, our linguistic capabilities develop further. Language also has a major influence on the development of brainpower. Children develop a "feel" for linguistics at the same pace as the development of their autobiographical memory. After all, many personal memories are recorded in words and concepts. If we do not speak the language yet, we cannot record situations in words. Language is the means by which we receive, store, and disseminate information. This book is an example of that.

The way you talk and the size of your vocabulary says something about your intelligence level. Conversely, language can also help you better understand the world around you. You often think in words, don't you? However, communication via language can also cause many problems. Not because it is that difficult to learn a certain language, but we often do not realize what the other person already knows and what their frame of reference is.

Regardless of how important language is for transferring information, it also causes many misunderstandings, particularly regarding emotions or other subjective matters. Language does not quite allow us to convey what we mean exactly.

What came first, thought or language? And are we able to express all thoughts in language? Whichever way you look at it, language fulfills an important function and continues to play an important role in modern means of communication, such as e-mail, blogs, and presentations.

Stenography or shorthand, a method for writing down spoken text at the same speed in which it is spoken, has existed for years. The little icons in chat and text messages are probably derived from the same urge. However, anyone is capable of developing their own shorthand. The purpose of abbreviations is to be able to represent information as concisely as possible, using just one single or a few letters or symbols. Many people, for example, draw up their weekly shopping list in their own, condensed code. When people collaborate closely, it is wise to agree on clear codes. It saves time and creates clearness: Each person knows what he or she has to do.

Gossips

For many people, the word "gossip" has an ugly ring to it. But gossip is actually an excellent way of communication, which we often underestimate. What did you last gossip about? Gossip is often about essential matters: relationships, family feuds, judgments. Many people love small talk and informal communication, precisely because these provide so much information. Gossiping is a spontaneous way of exchanging information in often pleasant surroundings. Our brain is susceptible to these two aspects.

Gossiping explains the success of virtual networks like Facebook, LinkedIn, MySpace, and the many blogs. Indeed, these are virtual ways of gossiping, but we have the same feeling of being in contact with others. However, we prefer talking to humans over talking to computers. Physical encounters and informal contacts are very important to us. To us, social interactions are a natural way of sharing information. The information ground theory (see Chapter 4) is based on this informal exchange of information.

Gossip conveys more than rumor. Rumors are improvised news items, but the moment at which you hear some gossip shows your position within a social network. It may be very revealing if you are the last to hear a particular piece of gossip.

Never underestimate the effect of gossip. It often contains meaty information. If you wish for certain information to reach everyone double-quick, then choose a person in your team who is able to spread information fast. Tell him or her the information as gossip, and you can be sure that everyone has heard your news by the end of the day.

Asking Questions

We raise our children, telling them to be especially curious. We prompt them to keep asking when there is something they don't understand. Often, though, managers are expected *not* to ask questions. After all, they know it all, don't they?

If you wish to receive good information, you will have to ask good questions. It is often more difficult than you think, and often you will get answers that you don't expect. Do not immediately forget the question you asked; see whether you really get an answer to your question.

People often do not know what question they must ask in order to get the right information. For example, if the context is not fully known, then getting the right information means asking clever questions to establish that context. Don't expect an immediate answer; ask opening questions to clarify what the other person is looking for. Using a few short questions and answers, you will quickly gain insight into the type of information the other person is seeking, whether you know the answer or the direction, and whether you are the right person to provide the needed information. Giving feedback to the inquirer is one of the main success factors for obtaining good information.

Some people often answer a question with another question. Often, they did not hear or understand the question properly, they are trying to play for time, or they simply have a habit of repeating other people's questions. Asking questions is a way of viewing your information from several viewpoints. This process will create new connections in your brain, and you will better remember the information. Only human beings are able to ask ourselves clever questions, as well as answer them.

When retrieving information, smart people search with the help of others. This is not because others know where you stored this information, but because they help your search behavior. They will ask you questions such as "what were you doing" or "where were you" when you got that information and stored it.

However, by simply asking questions, you can achieve an awful lot more. You pay attention to others, and thus receive a lot of information. A famous networker once told me that he had the ability to talk to any person, making it a pleasant experience for both. His secret was a simple one: He asks a maximum of five questions and then allows the other person to answer in full. He did not say which five questions he usually asks; he did not know this himself. But just by asking a few questions, you can soon find out what touches other people. In other words, the questions have to be aimed at the other person, not at you!

Better Communication

Understanding the information and communication profile of the recipient of our information will make or break our efforts at good communication. Often, we know who reads our communications but we do not tailor our message to these readers. For example, we almost always tell people more than we have to, even knowing that others are very busy, just like we are. Consider, for instance, a person who receives an e-mail from you, that will easily take two minutes to read. Longer messages will obviously take more time, and they become even more time-consuming when it is unclear whether and how the recipient has to react to your messages. Therefore, always phrase your message briefly and to the point; the other person will react more quickly.

The following list provides a few practical communication tips:

Sender

- Always take the recipient of your message into account. If you don't know the person well, try to find out more about him or her.
- Adjust each communication moment to the intellectual level of the user. Make sure that you know what that level is, and try to leave as little as possible to chance.
- E-mail is becoming increasingly more important. Make sure that the person to whom you are sending an e-mail knows after a few lines what is expected of them. If your e-mail is purely informative, then state this at the beginning.
- Information that is forced on others is sure to be less interesting than information they are looking out for. Seduce the user and give your e-mail message a catchy title.
- Make the information you are sending as personal as possible. Otherwise, you run the risk of having your information ignored quickly.
- Learn the art of storytelling. Storytelling trainer is an official profession. You could call on someone like that if you wanted to learn how to communicate a message convincingly.
- Check whether the recipient really needs your information. Avoid vague messages, messages that can be interpreted in many different ways, and purposeless information.
- Determine, for every message that you send, whether you would like to receive the information like that. In case of any doubts, don't

send the message. Should you ever receive a message like that, provide immediate feedback to the sender.
• Decide for yourself how many people you really owe information. The amount is often less than you think.

Recipient
• Train the sender. Let him or her know if you do not find e-mailing or chatting a pleasant way of communicating with them, or if you are annoyed by the content or thrust of their messages.
• Also, train your information producers (in other words, anyone who sends you, whether you asked for it or not, a lot of information).

Medium
• Check whether the means of communication you intend to use is the right medium for your message. Avoid sending e-mails with many and large attachments. It is better to post these in a joint electronic space.
• Instant messaging distracts many people during work. Use this medium sparingly, especially when you also e-mail intensively.
• Check in advance whether the recipient has sufficient knowledge of and skill for using the means of communication that you use for transferring your message.

Message
• Adapt your choice of words to your recipient. Do not underestimate or overestimate the other person's knowledge.
• Make clever use of signs and symbols. Nothing is as tiring as reading long lengths of text without any layout; use paragraphs, headings, and subheadings.
• Read every message that you are about to send once more before clicking *send*.
• Leave out unnecessary information. Keep your message concise and clear. The better you know the recipient, the shorter the message can be. Good communication means leaving out everything unnecessary.
• Show clearly who you are when you propagate a message. The recipient prefers to know whom they are dealing with. That is often the reason why they read your message.

- Remember that it is the recipient and not the sender who determines the effect of the message.
- Include, if possible, trust and reliability checks in your message. Most people are likely not to trust all disseminated information, based on personal experience. Help them to understand why your message is sound and worth reading.
- Carefully consider the subject of your message. Sometimes narrative messages are better received by a recipient. At other times, it is better to communicate your message by means of concise expressions or enumerations. Always consider how a recipient will be able to remember your message in the best possible way.

Of course, practice is the best teacher. Feel free to copy other people's communication techniques. As a team, regularly discuss communication as a part of everyone's information behavior.

STORYTELLING

Imagine that the art of printing had not been invented. Then we could only tell stories to each other. It could be the same story time and time again, but with slightly different emphases. Nearly everyone would be involved in this, all day long.

In prehistoric times, the ability to handle information skillfully was a necessity in order to survive. Where can we find food? How can we protect ourselves? Who is the enemy? Today, we still need comparable skills. However, something has changed, particularly in the last few years: the amount of information we collect.

Storytelling is nothing new. The Bible used it in abundance. Hollywood understood the principle of the storyteller right from the start. Our most important medium, television, also revolves around stories, from soap operas to documentaries and shows. Small children like to hear a story before they go to sleep. Parents add a lot of context to these in the shape of sounds and movements. But at a later age, stories are a source of information. For example, many popular books on management are the stories of successful managers.

Even when we are really old and live in a retirement home, stories may have their uses. Elderly people can easily become isolated unless you actively involve them in talking about the past. They can vividly remember the events from their youth and early adulthood. An afternoon spent talking to others about the old days, with or without moving pictures, evokes many memories and acts therapeutically. Studies show that in the very old, this even improves the functioning of their memory.

Oral Communication

It was not that long ago that we could transfer information only through speech. Even today, there are still groups of people who only transfer information via the spoken word. From our history books, it appears that the spoken word has great survival power. The disadvantage is, of course, that if a story is not written down, it is gone when the people who know it are no longer there.

Traditional tribes have developed remarkable techniques for exchanging information with each other and passing this information on to next generations. Take for example the Kope tribe,[1] which consists of around 5,000 people in Papua, New Guinea. The information that is exchanged is bound by certain customs and rules:

- *Dissemination*. News and gossip is needed, for example, for knowing where herds are or edible plants.
- *Induction*. Young people do not have access to all information. This is handed over by the elders. Only after this handing over do the young people become fully fledged members of the tribe.
- *Interpretation*. Information has to be useful. The hunters of the tribe use their eyes properly and look for clues in the landscape that show whether and in which direction their prey has moved.
- *Organization*. Information is shared for coordinating group activities such as the hunt or trade.
- *Presentation*. The manner in which information is represented has to fit with the goals and interests of all members of the tribe.
- *Preservation*. Especially the elders have to ensure that the cultural values and norms are preserved.

As a matter of fact, comparable rules also apply for any modern family, organization, or other association. The difference is that the members of the Kope tribe really do live according to these rules and that there is a lot of social control. That is not always the case in modern organizations. The members of modern organizations often work without any explicit rules, which means that many information exchanges do not go optimally.

Verbal Rules

When we can transfer information only by speech, it makes large demands on our memory. The fact is that our brain cannot store all that much information. For that reason, the members of the Kope tribe observe a few rules when they pass on information:

- All information is transferred in the vicinity of other members of the tribe. Communication takes place mainly within the same community, and information therefore rarely ends up with other groups.
- The members of the tribe use all kinds of memory techniques during the transfer of information, such as alliteration, rhyme, repetition, half-rhyme, nicknames, proverbs, and set expressions.
- They are capable of actively erasing memories, for example, because the information is no longer needed. When they no longer talk about information, the memory wears out.
- The tribal members tell each other information in a shape that immediately fits with their recipients. After all, the sender is informed of the level of knowledge and experience of virtually every other tribal member. Unnecessary information is simply left out.
- To new information, a few rules apply. It is transferred by elders, with the approval of the village elder, presented within the hierarchic structure of the community and (one reckons) with each other's opinion and the situation of that moment.
- Only skilled persons pass on the information.

Try to use these rules during your next communication moment.

Art of Storytelling

Information is best told in the shape of a story. Our brain is trained to remember this kind of information (see Chapter 3). Stories provide context, are often rich in detail, give meaning to dry facts, and leave room for personal interpretation. Stories fit in with already known information. Furthermore, if you tell your story directly to someone else, you will get an immediate reaction, even if it is just a smile.

Storytelling is an art that in large part can be learned. A storyteller has to come across as credible. A story is not an anecdote or a personal dream, but an authentic way of passing on information. If you wish to make sure that a story comes across properly and reliably, you have to bear in mind four elements:[2]

1. *The teller.* When telling a story, you wish to touch the listener's heart. You want to make room in their brain for recording your story. However, you can only touch their heart if you open up your own heart. Therefore, you should include your own emotions in your story.
2. *The audience.* The audience gives you time and attention. They want to have experienced or learned something after having heard your story. That means you have to fit your story into their background, interests, and emotions in that moment. Take your time to find out about these things when preparing your story.
3. *The moment.* A story is never the same. You constantly adjust it, for example, by means of the context of that particular moment. When telling your story, watch the faces of your audience carefully. Recognize emotions and assess what the audience really wishes to hear at that particular moment.
4. *The mission.* You wish to transfer information with your story, but what do you really want to achieve with it? In other words, ask yourself in advance what your goal is. Should your information instigate action? Or lead to new insights on certain subjects?

Conveying a message convincingly means telling a good story. However, very few get a professional to assist them with this. The problem is that few people know how to tell a story. But an even bigger problem is that even fewer people know that they do not know how to tell a story. For that reason, many managers take a thorough course in storytelling. It is seen as a basic skill for people who wish to enter the top 5 percent of an organization.

PICTURE PERFECT

People are mainly attuned to the visual. Our eyes process many facts, and those are important for assessing persons and situations. But no matter how well we are able to see, we must focus our attention if we wish to observe something in detail.

Looking seems easy enough, but appearances are deceptive. In spite of all its computing power and technical means, a computer is not capable of even approximating everything our visual senses can. Seeing and looking are two different things. We can all, for example, look at a painting, but to see what the painter really meant by it is a different story. Seeing means interpreting the visual information. As with stories, we have learned to supplement the missing parts of a picture, so we don't need all of the visual information to create an accurate image of reality.

Visualize

How can you see smarter? Visualizing is a known technique for seeing better, in which you imagine as best as possible what you wish to achieve. Athletes were among the first to embrace this technique. By visualizing each part of a complex movement, they convert these thoughts into automatic movements, something the brain loves. You too can use this technique in your work. By visualizing certain goals or actions in advance, you will notice that once you perform a visualized action, you learn certain actions quicker.

In a well-known experiment, the power of visualization techniques was examined. Two groups of people who had never played the piano before were both instructed on a piece of music. The music was played and the finger movements demonstrated. Next, one group was allowed to practice at the piano. The other group was asked to practice the piece in their head over the same period. Half way through the experiment, the brain activity of all test subjects was measured, and it turned out that both groups showed the same brain activity. Only toward the end did the group that was playing for real have a slight advantage. However, after the other group had been allowed to practice at the piano for a short period, they reached the same level very quickly.

Mindmapping

Mindmapping is another method for recording information in order to better remember it. These days, there are simple computer programs for mindmapping. The principle is based on the fact that we remember information better when the left and the right halves of the brain cooperate properly. A mindmap allows you to record all kinds of concepts in a schematic drawing using colors, lines, and patterns. The graphic elements are better remembered by the creative right side of your brain, while the analytical left side records the detailed information.

Mindmaps have another important advantage: They give us peace. Of course, it takes time to construct a figure, but once we start and keep our mind on it, peace will follow as a matter of course. We will not forget the end product quickly. After all, we do need much less data for recording our ideas. Finally, a drawing is much more appealing to our emotions than a list of separate words. This way, we make a strong connection with our memory.

Nowadays, it is also possible to provide insight into all digital communication flows using mindmapping software. The program shows the network of contacts and the traffic between different media in various ways. This information is very enlightening because this helps us to recall with whom we communicated and on what subjects. Such a schematic representation of messages provides us, as it were, with a story.

Picture This

Everyone who has ever looked at the financial pages of a newspaper knows that it takes a lot of effort to keep your mind on these seemingly boring articles. This could be improved. Knowing that your brain sees every letter as an image, you understand that to our brain words are therefore the same as a whole lot of images. That explains why we are unable to read words really quickly but can digest a picture at high speed.

When we create a picture, we first have to interpret the information before being able to reproduce it. We have to combine the information, put it together, and distribute it differently. A picture says a lot more than words, particularly because it allows us to transfer information differently.

The advantage of a picture is that we can take in information in a single blink of an eye. Seeing a picture, we often don't need to even think, because it immediately fits in with our visual memory. A good image 1) shows information at different levels, 2) invites us to think about its contents, 3) invites our eyes to compare the various part of the image to each other, and most importantly 4) initiates action.

If you wish to improve your observation skills, then involve all your senses. Be aware of what you hear, smell, and feel when you look at something. Your sense of time will also change. The more senses you involve when observing, the richer and longer the time will seem to be when you remember that moment. Compare, for example, an hour in a doctor's waiting room and an hour's visit to a museum. Furthermore, attentively looking at things improves your mood. When your brain is actively set to work, it experiences these moments as joyful.

Imagine

Why do we actually take photographs? Is it so that we can see in ten or twenty years what we have experienced? By that time, do we actually need to do so? Do we know now what photos we will want to see by then?

Photos are taken as reminders. Memories are about the past, but we evoke them in the present. In reality, reminders of, for example, how we experienced a party, may be far removed from the truth. In that case, our memory is a subjective version of recollections and digital artifacts. The real experience of the event has disappeared behind the external souvenir, such as a photo.

An increasing number of people put their information online. It is particularly true that young people are not sufficiently aware of the fact that you lose control over any information that you put on-line. They do not realize that their photos, sometimes even modified, end up on sites where they probably would not like them to be seen.

It is evitable that digital media are modified. We can touch up our own photos and this way influence and embellish our external photo memory. However, there is a danger of false memories. Do we remember the manipulated photos or the real event?

It seems as if we remember more than in the past. These days, we have photos and videos of almost every event in our lives. Digital media are not the reason for a better memory, but they do affect our ability to remember more details of specific events. Moreover, because photos and videos are often made on special occasions, we remember these events better. Our brain loves change. Information that deviates from the norm to our brain is information that we remember better.

If you wish to remember a certain situation well, then focus your attention. You can take a real photo, but often it is also possible to take a mental picture of a situation or information that you wish to remember well. Take an extra-long look at that situation. You will notice that you are much more able to visualize this situation or information, and therefore much more able to remember it.

NAVIGATING THE INFORMATION SEA

There are many similarities between finding your way in a big city and searching on the Internet. In a city, you look for street signs; on a Web site, you look for labels, buttons, or other symbols. When exploring a city on foot, you have plenty of time to read the names of streets or even walk back a few yards. If you have plenty of time, you can read each Web site or periodical at your leisure. When you are in a hurry, you wish to end up in the right place quickly. Both in the city and on Web sites, we like structure, although not excessively so. When a structure is so complex that it needs extra information to dissect it, it overshoots itself.

By the way, there is no need for a structure to square with reality. Think, for example, of the London Underground map. The map was designed as early as 1933, and provides insight into the location of and relation between the stations and, for example, the river Thames. The information on that map is not entirely correct. In the center, designer Harry Beck used a fixed distance between stations and only straight lines and diagonals at an angle of 45 degrees. The map leaves out virtually all details above ground and is not to scale. The strength of his design lies especially in its clarity and simplicity.

The information on the London Underground map fits in wonderfully well with the way in which we orient ourselves. We only need landmarks for finding our way. Furthermore, that simplified representation of reality demands less memory capacity. By remembering such a cognitive map, we can also follow the routes on this map in our mind's eye. In our brain, positions and distances are also relative and never geometrically exact. The abovementioned mindmaps also fit in nicely with a subway map.

In the Netherlands in 2005, an experiment was conducted in which a busy junction was stripped of virtually all notices, markings, and other traffic signs. The idea behind this was simple: Everything that could distract the road user was left out. Physical objects, like speed bumps, crosswalks, and curbs were removed. Because of these measures, the junction is a now lot safer and the traffic flow has improved. How is that possible?

Road users are accustomed to signs and other directions on the road. When these are removed, they have to pay extra attention. Drivers slow down and more often make eye contact with other road users, for example, pedestrians wishing to cross. We can certainly steer our behavior. That is worth remembering when you provide information: Put less information on a screen, and show only information that is important at that particular moment. The rest is just surplus noise. Something worth considering the next time you have to present large amounts of information.

I told you before that the context of an event is important to our memory. How often have you heard people say that they can remember exactly where they were when hearing about a major event? Or that they know where they last saw a certain person, but they've forgotten his or her name? Storage of extra three-dimensional context will help a memory surface quicker. Therefore, if you wish to better remember information, it is a good idea to actively record the space in which the event took place.

In the preface of this book, I specified that you should take the time to study the table of contents in advance. This approach helps you make a mental classification of the book and will enable you to find information more quickly. By making a mental table of contents and visualizing the chapters or parts, you give your brain more interesting information to remember. Next, you will even be able to leaf through the book in your mind's eye and retrieve this information.

NOTES

1. Madden, A. D., Bryson, J., & Palimi, J. (2006). Information behavior in pre-literate societies. In: Spink, A. & Cole, C. (Eds.). *New Directions in Human Information Behavior.* Dordrecht: Springer.
2. Guber, P. (2007). The four truths of the storyteller. *Harvard Business Review, 85*(12), 52–59.

CHAPTER 11

━━━━━

PEOPLE AT WORK

The human brain is a social brain. We like to talk to other people, we love other people, and we need other people to live a happy life. In all this, information plays an increasingly important role. This section mainly revolves around the question: What do you want and need to know?

Choosing from the large information supply is like choosing from people that you meet and get to know better. There are more than six billion people walking this Earth. Ultimately, you will only get to know a few of them well. Many others will come and go. It is the same with information. Ultimately, there will only be a few subjects that you wish to know more about because they interest you. The rest are not useful enough to store in your memory.

In this last chapter, I will provide recommendations on how to set up that network of people, how you can manage information workers, and especially on how to grow old inquisitively.

SMART PEOPLE

The very best way to obtain good information is via other people. They know you, it will cost you little time and effort to assign them your query, and you will be able to immediately respond to the information they bring you. Furthermore, by asking you extra questions, they will be able to find out much better what you wish to know. A five-minute conversation usually yields more information than a five-hour search on the Internet. It is therefore important to get in touch and keep in touch with people who can provide you with the right information.

People love sharing information with others. When a colleague asks you for information, agree under the following conditions:

- *Reciprocity*. You do something for me and I will do something for you. Or someone else that you know. You expect a service in return in the near future.
- *Reputation*. If you are seen as an expert or a guru, you expect nothing in return. The sheer fact that you are asked affirms your status, time and time again.
- *Altruism*. They do still exist: colleagues who do things without expecting anything in return. People often think that providing others with information is a reward in itself.

Successful networking means knowing the personal profiles of others who present themselves on that network. After all, everyone has a unique information profile (see Chapter 5). If there is no profile for your network, then have one done for everyone at the same time and share the results. The advantages are obvious.

Beyond the Yellow Pages

In some organizations, the Who's Who pages are used intensively. These pages include not just the phone numbers and addresses of all employees but also up-to-the-minute information on them, such as their current projects and activities, for example. Furthermore, all details are automatically synchronized with data from systems such as the staff database and the projects administration. It has to be possible for everyone to change their own data at any time. It is also important for everyone to check regularly whether their own data is still up to date. Whether you are new to the organization, making contact with others, or selecting new people for your project, these pages provide you with good basic information.

It is ever smarter to include the ambition level and personal interests of a worker. After all, when selecting employees for a new project, you wish to select those who are ready to take the next step in their career. Personal information in a profile has a positive effect when approaching someone, even when you don't know that person.

You can also make use of these Who's Who pages when appraising your employees. How well does someone keep their profile in such a network updated? Do they like sharing information with others? Do they answer other's questions quickly and well? Do they refer to good experts? Are they actively involved in discussions that are important to the organization?

Ensure sufficient variations in the personal network of your team members. People who have known each other for a long time often don't feel open to or see the necessity of getting to know others. The network deteriorates as a result. Many employees are still put off by someone's position, background, department, or availability. Obligation is not an option, but suggest to them, for example, that they have lunch with others to discuss a topical issue.

Selecting People

How do you decide which people are a valuable addition to your information network? The next list indicates why you select a person when you need information. You select a person because he or she . . .

- Is known to you; also because you think that person knows enough others.
- Has a lot of knowledge and in the past has proved to be a good and reliable information source.
- Is willing to share knowledge. This person is easily approachable, a good listener, and answers quickly, even if he or she doesn't know the answer.
- Is straightforward, inspires confidence, and gives honest advice.
- Has a similar position or matches you in education and experience.
- Is close to you. We still prefer to choose someone in our immediate physical proximity.
- Has better access, in your opinion, to particular information sources.

- Has intuition and insight and can easily empathize with your position.
- Gets things done more quickly than going through formal, often bureaucratic, methods.
- Will keep certain information informal, such as clinical pictures or a financial crisis, for example.
- Is a good storyteller and is always informed of the latest news.
- Is just one level higher up in the organization.
- Likes to show off his or her knowledge. Asking a question of this person will help you earn easy prestige with them.

And sometimes, we ask others for information simply because it is easier to have others do the work.

However, not everybody finds it easy to approach someone when they need information. There are often different causes for this:

- *The time that you have known the person.* Whether you have known someone a long or a short time reveals something about the turnover within an information network.
- *The person's accessibility.* People like to cooperate closely with others who are physically near. If you wish to reach someone virtually, they have to be easy to find and quickly accessible.
- *The person's position within the organization.* People sometimes believe their organization is flat, but the position that someone holds within a company often plays a part in their contact with others, certainly when sharing information.
- *The part of the organization that you belong to.* In larger companies, departments or business units only sporadically mutually share their information.
- *Resemblance.* Is the other person a bit like you? For our information network, we mainly seek like-minded people with comparable experience, lifestyle, education, or background.
- *Time.* Does the other person have time for you? Or does this person give you attention exactly because he or she has too much time on his/her hands? (This person may not be the best informer.)
- *The time it takes to find the answer via another person.* Would it not be better to find the answer to your question yourself?

Analyze Your Network

For your own benefit, draw up a network analysis of your immediate working environment. In doing so, concentrate on sharing information within that network. Ask yourself the following questions:

- Who provides you with the information for doing your job?
- Is that person the best choice for the information that you need?
- Do I pass information to the right people?
- Do I have access to the right person when I need information?
- Am I comfortable enough to share that information with that person?

You can expand on these answers by including aspects such as time and money in the relationship.

The next step is checking out how you can improve this network: Add or remove people, maintain relationships better, pass on better quality information, and so on. Talk to a real networker and learn about his or her experiences and approach. Present this person with a concrete issue or personal problem and ask how to tackle it.

MANAGING INFORMATION WORKERS

The number of people just working with their brains is growing steadily. Currently, three in four employees are real information workers. Even traditional production workers are increasingly working with information. Knowledge workers are allowed to, even have to, think during office hours. They have to invent new products or applications, bring people together, or optimize existing business processes. With the number of new technologies and as many young people dealing with information in a different way, many managers are justly wondering how to steer everybody's information behavior in the right direction.

Managers who delegate more show that they trust their employees. They also use the capacities of their workers. However, you often see that people are not optimally deployed. One way is to tell people what they may expect and when. Expectations can determine whether you see or don't see information. If an employee recognizes the right information, dopamine is released, which in turn favors clear and creative thinking. However, Rock[1] discovered more from research. People get even higher levels of dopamine with *unanticipated* positive outcomes. Moreover, negative outcomes when expected positive ones results in low levels of dopamine. This shows that expectation can indeed affect your information productivity.

Another way open to managers is the so-called *walkabout*: walking around and talking to people to find out what gives. It is beneficial to our physical constitution, a good way of gathering news, and good for our cognitive powers.

Walkabouts are originally an Australian aboriginal tradition: young adults discover themselves during a long journey across unknown territory. When managers go on the shop floor, this is also often unknown territory to them. A walkabout can be useful for reestablishing the contact with the shop floor and is strongly recommended in times of crisis within an organization.

Based on Davenport,[2] here are some specific recommendations for achieving the right information behavior in knowledge workers. First, a manager must create communities, virtual teams in which like-minded people do the same work. Such a team is mainly created as a social network for distributing knowledge. The manager's task is to set up, facilitate, and cherish these virtual teams. They also have to ensure sufficient overlap between the various teams. This guarantees an even better exchange of information.

Second, a manager needs to ensure that the best information workers are recruited and retained. An organization has to make the right efforts for making information work attractive.

Third, attention is required to develop information skills in knowledge workers. A manager must not assume in advance that everybody is skilled in search techniques, means of collaboration, or the latest technologies. He or she needs to encourage people to continuously learn from each other and simultaneously pass on acquired knowledge to the other team members. People who keep knowledge and expertise to themselves are, by definition, not good team workers.

Fourth, a larger involvement of the knowledge worker in his department's decision-making processes is conducive to a close-knit team. Furthermore, a manager can provide opportunities for participating in external networks, which ultimately also benefit the organization.

Fifth, you have to challenge information workers. If they come to you with a problem but without any initiative for a solution, you should immediately send them away. They must at least have thought about a solution. Often, they will return the next day with an approach to their problem. Their brain has indeed worked overtime during the night.

Finally, a manager must allow knowledge workers to grow in the sharing of information by giving specific guidelines and directions. A knowledge worker does not need too much structure, but the right individual attention to their information behavior will allow a manager to achieve a lot.

Currently, managing (or in fact supervising) information workers is one of the hardest management tasks. Make sure to maintain a continuous dialogue with these highly skilled professionals. Act as a good sounding board at an intrinsic and relational level.

Manager as Information Worker

In spite of all of the changing organizational structures and up-and-coming social networks, the manager is still ultimately responsible for the results of his or her team. A manager's most important task is making many decisions. To this purpose, a manager needs information to reduce the uncertainty under which he or she makes those decisions. But the question remains: Where does a manager get all this information? Which information sources, including the people around him or her, will the manager consult?

Every manager needs two types of information: 1) hard information, which is processed quantitatively, and 2) soft information, which mainly consists of ideas, opinions, and images, but also includes gossip and vague suppositions. Every manager has a preference for verbal information, because it allows the information giver to provide lots of context. A manager receives a lot of information but is also constantly looking for better information. This is a paradox: The manager is at the limit of having too much information, but still does not get quite enough information.

Because of the speed at which change occurs, managers simply no longer have sufficient time to do everything themselves. That is why their information network is so important. The people around managers are and remain their main information sources. The adage "it is not what you know but who you know" is still applicable. Perhaps it used to be just laziness when managers made a major appeal to the specialists surrounding them. These days, it really is absolutely essential to call in experts.

Information Behavior of Managers

Because the information behavior of managers is different, a few propositions for optimally using each other's knowledge and skill in the application and use of information are explored below:

- A manager prefers verbal, visual, time-related, and aggregated information. Teach your workers your preferences.
- A manager is almost always informed of new information sources later than the experts. Knowledge of the existence of particular sources often involves a high degree of coincidence. Direct that coincidence by reading the right journals and particularly by talking to people and by ensuring that you regularly add new people to your network. Ask and keep asking your team members whether they know any interesting sources.
- Draw up a network analysis purely for your own benefit. Recognition of the main people of the information flows around you is the first step toward improving your information behavior.
- Managers initially select a person as an information source because they know the person, trust him/her, or simply like him/her, not because the person has specific knowledge. A manager often works against the clock. Someone who knows the manager well will have a better idea of the information needed by that manager.
- A manager knows that a reliable source of information is very important. If they have to incur extra high costs to maintain the source, they simply put up with it.

Information Behavior of Groups

The information behavior of groups of people is currently being researched.[3] The Internet has brought about new types of information behavior, such as wikis and blogs. The results of the first studies show that there are still many differences between people in a group, as far as familiarity and experience with information sources are concerned. We also know that the lack of specific knowledge incites people to collaborate with others. The lack of access, an information request that is too large or complex for one single person, and the fact that all sorts of information sources are too spread out are other reasons for people to collaborate.

However, we do not know all that much about the information behavior of a group of people. We do know that many employees would rather cooperate in relatively small teams and exchange a great deal of information, such as in operating theaters, boardrooms, or cockpits. The fact is that in one single location, all information flows and management skills come together: in the cockpit of an airplane. Pilots work against the clock, have to base their decisions on incomplete information, and always have several alternatives from which only one can be chosen. The cockpit is the classic example of a small group of experts in a small room being responsible for the lives of hundreds of people.

Currently, flying is the safest means of transportation.[4] Flying on a commercial plane has a fatality rate of 0.04 per 100 million passenger miles; compare this to driving, which has a fatality rate of 0.86. Two measures have contributed to this. First, the introduction of the flight simulator: A pilot can gain experience without this costing any human life or planes. By training in all types of unique, lifelike situations, the brain's decision centers are well fed with information and with this knowledge and wisdom. Some management teams use training in flight simulators to be teach their teams how to make decisions better and more quickly as a group.

Second, based on a NASA study, a system was introduced in which the power of the captain was breached. Previously, many accidents happened because captains made decisions without properly consulting their colleagues. The new system provides an environment in which everybody's opinion, even if it is conflicting, is considered and weighed. For good reason, this solution has also been introduced in, for example, operating theaters.

Gender in the Brain

Everyone occasionally suffers from information stress, but brain research has demonstrated that women are much better able to handle such an emotionally charged situation. They will also resign themselves sooner, instead of reacting aggressively.

The female brain uses, on average, 15 percent more blood than the male brain. In the brain, there is a clearly visible difference between gray matter and white matter. Gray matter consists of the cell bodies of the neurons; white matter consists of the nerve fibers (axons) that connect the neurons across long distances. On average, women have 55 percent gray matter, men 50 percent. Gray matter is synonymous with, for example, language and verbal aptitude. Female brains have more space between neurons, which means more connections. Two key language centers are larger in females than in males, giving women the edge when learning to talk.

By contrast, men have more white matter than women. White matter takes information to remote areas in the brain. This possibly explains why men have more visual/spatial capacities. Male brains are 8 to 10 percent bigger and more densely packed with neurons. Males also excel at reasoning out a problem.

Men and women also differ from each other with regard to acquiring, processing, and disseminating information. A few points are listed:

Women	Men
Have very good language skills	Are better at storing organized information
Are better at remembering incoherent word sequences	Are often better at assessing distances and directions
Have a wider perspective	Do not need all information for a decision, but trust their own judgment
Are better at recognizing faces	
Pay more attention to landmarks	Seek the information they need themselves
Take in information from different sources before making a decision	Sooner provide information and criticism
Research received information in fairly great detail	Immediately seek the solution to a problem, often without checking first whether there is indeed a problem

Women	Men
Have more imagination and intuition	Do not admit quickly to not knowing
Are more sensitive to colors and details	something
Read a lot of information by using	Particularly systematize (i.e., analyze and
intuition and enhanced social skills, and	devise organizational categories)
by interpreting facial expressions	Rather look at information from one single
Look at information from several	perspective
perspectives	Work on one single information problem
Better understand nonverbal expressions	at the same time, analyze it, take care of
Are capable of performing several	a solution, and then continue with the
information tasks simultaneously, because	next problem
their left and right brain better cooperate	Prefer looking for information individually
Are better at remembering words and	Are impatient when they need to seek
symbols, because they record more	information
emotions with events	Are more quickly satisfied with the results
Will ask for help much sooner when	of their search for information
searching for information	Almost always want information for
Are more open to collaboration	nothing
Are patient when they do not immediately	
find certain information	
Have no trouble paying for good	
information	

Men are supposed to have more affinity with technology. That conclusion is confirmed every day when you look around you. However, women appear to be just as capable of using technology; they simply do not demonstrate this as easily in a public place. When using a source like the Internet, men are also inclined to give their opinion on it from a technical point of view. Women simply *use* the Internet, without saying too much about it.

These studies show that men use information and IT predominantly for their own work and mutual competition. Women use information and IT for creating a profile for themselves, for personal commitment, for cooperation, and for understanding the situation better. The latter is particularly important for women: They like to create a story within the right context using the information they have found.

Of course, emphasizing one single characteristic when explaining information behavior is biased. However, knowing these differences does help to start a process of change.

New Jobs

These days, many employees' main job is to collect, process, and disseminate information. This emphasis on information has created new jobs, with the main purpose of using these to an organization's competitive advantage.

An *information professional* focuses on improving access to information and the quality of information. To that purpose, information professionals design information products and services that help teams function better. In this respect, think of information managers, Web content specialists, or project officers.

A *gatekeeper* is an employee who coordinates information flows within an organization. A gatekeeper is also very well-informed of what goes on outside an organization. Gatekeepers collect information, emphasize information, or even suppress information. They are key people between the organization and all its stakeholders. A gatekeeper not only provides information but also provides practical advice.

An *infomediary* takes things a step further. This person, who is often part of an external organization, collects, analyzes, and processes information and resells this commercially. Sometimes these are true information brokers who bring together information demand and supply.

Nowadays, the single most important factor in organizations is information literacy. Information literacy is defined as a set of abilities: being able to recognize when information is needed as well as being able to locate, evaluate, and use it effectively. Only when a person recognizes his or her own information behavior and that of those in his or her information network can that person take the right steps toward improving the way information is acquired, analyzed, and disseminated.

It is against this background that a new and important information function is emerging: the *information coach*. The information coach helps employees understand and improve their information behavior. The coach does this in three ways: 1) by assessing the best information environment for an organization; 2) by providing assistance to managers and employees in selecting the best training and support organization for their behavioral information issues; and 3) by identifying the information profile of employees and recommending improvements they can make to become information literate and productive.

One of the reasons for this new function is the fact that an increasing number of organizations are becoming dependent on reliable, timely, and accurate information. An organization also has to balance compliance responsibilities with confidentiality; new technologies can help by giving organizations more fine-grained control over the collection, management, and security of their information. Another reason is that the average employee is insufficiently information literate. New tools to manage information require a new way of working for many information workers, yet not many have been trained in using them. The older generation is only just catching up with the tools and practices of today's information work.

We all know which colleague, friend, or relative we need to ask to get an answer to our question or problem. However, we do not use that person until the problem or question occurs. I often advise managers to use that clever colleague as an information coach; ask them to walk around *actively* for one hour per week and help everyone with tips and tricks. That clever colleague does know you, so the help will be geared to your knowledge level. After all, people particularly learn from each other. Everybody has his or her own clever solution, which will find its way throughout the organization and into society this way. The effect of that one-hour investment is that your colleagues truly increase their productivity. Additionally, it can be highly motivating, and there is an immediate reward for both parties.

TIMING IS EVERYTHING

Time is a scarce item in our Western society. Most people lack time. We cannot purchase or hire extra time, nor can we store it for later use. There is no substitute for time. Our sense of time is learned, not innate.

Because our time is limited, our attention is also limited—and because of the increasing quantity of information sources, our attention is more fragmented than ever. Linda Stone, formerly at Microsoft, coined the term *continuous partial attention* as early as 1998 to describe the tendency to constantly divide one's attention between the real and the virtual world. There is so much information we would like to give our attention to, but we have to make choices. We also need to decide in which order we wish to give things attention. The wider the difference in the information tasks we have to perform, the more time it takes to deal with information. One clever approach is to divide the time that we spend on a specific task into larger chunks. We have a lot of trouble if we divide our attention over many different items. Each time, we need to pick up where we left off, and that takes time.

When you keep an eye on how you spend your time, you will have more time left. How can you assess the things on which you spend your valuable time? An important step is to concentrate on information tasks, such as seeking information, finding the right people for answering your questions, and the use of technology for finding information or for remembering what you once knew.

Furthermore, our brain needs time to process information. We therefore need moments to reflect, during which we select which signs are worth being stored. Complex information tasks, such as writing a report or preparing for an exam, will take up much more time. "Last-minute" types are always at a disadvantage, because their brain does not get sufficient opportunity to weigh, rearrange, and powerfully store information again (during the night, for example).

Morning people and night owls each have their own rhythms. Early birds have a 24-hour rhythm; night owls are closer to 25 hours. Our biological clock runs around a second per day faster—in other words, around six minutes per year. That explains why many people, as they get older, start to behave more like early birds. They get up earlier and go to bed earlier. Perhaps that is why, as we get older, we feel that time is running faster. We have to adjust our biological clock more often with the physical time, and that becomes harder each day. Older people have more trouble adjusting to night shifts and intercontinental flights.

Incidentally, our society is mainly geared to early birds. That is not convenient for young people, whose internal clock we know is an hour behind adults. Nevertheless, classes and lectures often start early. Not all that effective.

When you have to process a lot of new information over a period of time, you should take a break and get sufficient rest. Not because your body needs it, but because your brain needs time to make all these new connections.

The same companies that supply us with all kinds of technical tools for bombarding each other with information also provide possible solutions against this *information overload*. The software and hardware company Intel, for example, recently presented a study into the best way of helping their employees to handle all sorts of digital interruptions. As a result of this study, every Tuesday morning, all possible nuisances are as much as possible avoided: e-mail and chat programs are turned off, "do not disturb" signs are placed on doors, no meetings are scheduled, and so on. The objective is to create a few hours of real thinking time once a week. And it does work!

In some countries, it is almost an obligation to have an afternoon tea break. Japan has a true tea culture, but in Germany and Great Britain, this break is also institutionalized. Of course, you don't necessarily have to take a tea break. A reading break, brief nap, a few breathing exercises, a chat, or listening to music help you relax mentally.

Before making a difficult decision with serious consequences, you are well-advised to sleep on it. Just before going to sleep, write on a notepad what you need or wish to decide on the next day. Writing is a powerful method of putting your brain to work. During the night, your brain will categorize the day's information, sort it out, and store it again. The next morning, you will have all this information more neatly arranged at your disposal.

Another technique is to slow your intake of information. Read more slowly, take the speed out of conversations with others, and ask those sending information to just tell you the basics. It is quite an art, because we love to tell everything we know. The best teachers or presenters are those who include frequent and lengthy pauses in their speech. They know that the brain needs time to digest new information.

And what would you think about an *information sabbatical*? During that period, you use no e-mail, Internet, or phone. You also receive no news, watch no television, and do not read any newspapers or journals. The world will keep turning anyway. Plan such a period well in advance. That way, you have something to look forward to, and your environment can bear it in mind. Restore any possible "damage" directly after that period, by talking to a close colleague or good friend and asking them what they think you have missed. Next, take action to experience the sense of freedom of this "information fast" more often. Most people value such an information sabbatical and do not begrudge others such a period.

SEASONED CITIZENS

Everyone discovers that certain memory tasks take more effort when we grow older. We have more trouble remembering new information, recalling names and words, concentrating on something, or learning new things. We process information more slowly, our ability to respond decreases, and we have more difficulty performing several tasks simultaneously. Many people are haunted by the prospect of memory deterioration.

Although the memory gets worse as we grow older, two essential characteristics of our mental life remain intact: higher order language and perception. We all know writers and journalists who are active until a very old age. The elderly are able to effortlessly place new or unknown objects, matters, or concepts in a broader framework. They recognize a number of common characteristics and are thus able to rapidly categorize something new or unknown.

Moreover, recent research has taught us that in older people, procedural memory does not deteriorate. That memory contains the knowledge needed for solving everyday problems. Therefore, an older employee can still perform well. Architect Frank Lloyd Wright designed the Guggenheim Museum at the age of 90! At the same time, older people tend to become more relaxed. They have gained life experience, which makes them react less violently to new situations. They have seen it all before.

People who are getting on in years do benefit from techniques that improve retrieval of information. A number of tips include:

- *Change.* New surroundings mean new stimuli for the brain. Staying in the same environment does not provide any new impulses, and that might bore your brain.
- *Create context.* This is the most important advice that can be given to anyone. Store as much context as possible with information that you wish to remember. Look, listen, smell, experience, communicate attentively, and store everything actively. In a quiet moment, ascertain your impressions of that moment. Relive the situation.

- *Dare.* You do not need to wear or follow the fashion or the music of young people, but you can appreciate them. Read a magazine for the young or check out a blog just to see what makes them tick.
- *De-stress.* This does not apply only to older people. Psychological pressure, depressions, and other emotional problems lessen the ability to properly process information. It is also better to avoid negative people.
- *Eat healthy.* A good eating pattern contributes to a healthy life-style. Anything goes, provided it is in moderation.
- *Exercise.* Especially as you get older, sufficient exercise is impor-tant. Physical activity will help the blood flow better and bring more energy to the brain.
- *First, try it yourself.* Each person, no matter what age, is often more capable than he or she thinks. It is not a bad starting point to first try to find the right information yourself, before asking others for help.
- *Laugh.* When you laugh, dopamine is released, providing much-needed relaxation. Humor provides context and helps us remember information more easily. Dopamine also helps us perform cognitive tasks better.
- *Network.* Do not allow your social contacts to disintegrate. Your network of family, friends, and acquaintances is of vital impor-tance to an active lifestyle.
- *Play.* Card games, as well as puzzles and video games, promote the generation of new connections.
- *Sleep.* Sleep really helps. The benefits of taking a nap during the day have been proven. Meditate, if it makes you feel better.
- *Slow down.* Be sure not to take in too much information in one go. Insert sufficient breaks to give your brain a chance to store all (new) information properly.
- *Stay curious.* To young people, lifelong learning is the natural thing to do, but old people would also do well to continue learn-ing. There is no need to learn a new language or study when you are old, but do make sure that you keep informed of any new developments around you.
- *Wish.* Do what you always wanted to do. When you retire, you will have an awful lot of time. Follow your heart: write, paint, travel. Everything you do with enthusiasm is intrinsically rewarding.

Older people have learned that entering into relations with other people results in becoming well-informed. They also know what interests them and let the rest simply go by.

A large number of studies have shown that the brain adjusts itself to the input it receives. The more information, the more variation, the less chance of dementia or memory diseases. The main measure we can take to ensure that we can continue to process information to a ripe old age is simply selection. Select those knowledge areas and subjects that you would like information on, and leave the rest to others.

The information mountain will grow more than we can foresee right now. With so much information available, only the information that we really make our own is important. People who have the ability to select what is important to them are the most prepared for the decades to come.

NOTES

1. Rock, D. (2009). *Your brain at work: Strategies for overcoming distraction, regaining focus, and working smarter all day long.* New York: HarperBusiness.
2. Davenport, T. (2005). *Thinking for a living: How to get better performance and results from knowledge workers.* Boston: Harvard Business Press.
3. Hyldegård, J. (2009). Beyond the search process: Exploring group members' information behavior in context. *Information Processing & Management, 45*(1), 142–158.
   Talja, S. & Hansen, P. (2006). Information sharing. In: Spink, A. & Cole, C. (Eds.). *New Directions in Human Information Behavior.* Dordrecht: Springer.
4. Lehrer, J. (2009). *How we decide.* Boston: Houghton Mifflin Harcourt.

REFERENCES

Aamodt, S. & Wang, S. (2008). *Welcome to your brain: Why you lose your car keys but never forget how to drive and other puzzles of everyday life*. New York: Bloomsbury USA.

Abbott, R. D. (1999). *The world as information: Overload and personal design*. Bristol: Intellect Books.

Allen, D. (2008). *Making it all work: Winning at the game of work and the business of life*. New York: Viking Adult.

Bawden, D., Holtham, C., & Courtney, N. (1999). Perspectives on information overload. *ASLIB Proceedings*, 51(8), 249–255.

Begley, S. (2007). *Train your mind, change your brain: How a new science reveals our extraordinary potential to transform ourselves*. New York: Ballantine Books.

Bell, G. & Gemmell, J. (2009). *Total recall: How the e-memory revolution will change everything*. New York: Dutton Adult.

Blakeslee, S. & Blakeslee, M. (2007). *The body has a mind of its own: How body maps in your brain help you do (almost) everything better*. New York: Random House Trade Paperbacks.

Brandhof, J. W. (2008). *The business brain book: Work smarter, save time*. Maastricht: BrainWare.

Brizendine, L. (2006). *The female brain.* New York: Broadway Books.

Case, D. O. (2002). *Looking for information: A survey of research on information seeking, needs, and behavior.* San Diego: Academic Press.

Cross, R. & Parker, A. (2004). *The hidden power of social networks: Understanding how work really gets done in organizations.* Boston, MA: Harvard Business Press.

Davenport, T. (2005). *Thinking for a living: How to get better performances and results from knowledge workers.* Boston, MA: Harvard Business School Press.

Décosterd, M. L. (2008). *Right brain/left brain leadership: Shifting style for maximum impact.* Westport, CT: Praeger Publishers.

Devlin, K. (2001). *Infosense: Turning information into knowledge.* New York: W.H. Freeman and Company.

Dijck, J. van (2007). *Mediated memories: Personal cultural memory in the digital age.* Stanford, CA: Stanford University Press.

Dispenza, J. (2008). *Evolve your brain: The science of changing your mind.* Deerfield Beach, FL: Health Communications, Inc.

Doidge, N. (2007). *The brain that changes itself: Stories of personal triumph from the frontiers of brain science.* New York: Viking Adult.

Edmunds, A. & Morris, A. (2000). The problem of information overload in business organizations: A review of the literature. *International Journal of Information Management, 20*(1), 17–28.

Eppler, M. & Mengis, J. (2004). The concept of information overload: A review of literature from organization science, accounting, marketing, MIS, and related disciplines. *The Information Society, 20*(5), 325–344.

Feather, J. (2004). *The information society: A study of continuity and change.* London: Facet Publishing.

Fine, C. (2006). *A mind of its own: How your brain distorts and deceives.* New York: W. W. Norton & Co.

Finkelstein, S., Whitehead, J., & Campbell, A. (2009). *Think again: Why good leaders make bad decisions and how to keep it from happening to you.* Boston: Harvard Business School Press.

Fisher, K. E., Erdelez, S., & McKechnie, E. F. (Eds.) (2005). *Theories of information behavior: A researcher's guide.* Medford, NJ: Information Today.

Garreau, J. (2006). *Radical evolution: The promise and peril of enhancing our minds, our bodies—and what it means to be human.* New York: Broadway Books.

Gazzaniga, M. S. (2008). *Human: The science behind what makes us unique*. New York: HarperCollins Publishers.

Gilkey, R. & Kilts, C. (2007). Cognitive fitness. *Harvard Business Review*, 85(11), 53–66.

Goldberg, E. (2006). *The wisdom paradox—How your mind can grow stronger as your brain grows older*. New York: Gotham.

Goldberg, E. (2009). *The new executive brain: Frontal lobes in a complex world*. Oxford: Oxford University Press.

Greenfield, S. (2004). *Tomorrow's people: How 21st-century technology is changing the way we think and feel*. London: Penguin Books.

Greenfield, S. (2008). *ID: The quest for identity in the 21st century*. London: Sceptre.

Hale-Evans, R. (2006). *Mind performance hacks: Tips & tools for overclocking your brain*, Sebastopol, CA: O'Reilly Media.

Hallowell, E. M. (2007). *Crazy busy: Overstretched, overbooked, and about to snap! Strategies for handling your fast-paced life*. New York: Ballantine Books.

Horstman, J. (2009). *The Scientific American day in the life of your brain*. New York: Jossey-Bass.

Hurst, M. (2007). *Bit literacy: Productivity in the age of information and e-mail overload*. New York: Good Experience Press.

Iacoboni, M. (2009). *Mirroring people: The new science of how we connect with others*. New York: Farrar, Strauss and Giroux.

Ibarra, H. & Lineback, K. (2005). What's your story? *Harvard Business Review*, 83(1), 64–71.

Jacobs, C. S. (2009). *Management rewired: Why feedback doesn't work and other surprising lessons from the latest brain science*. New York: Portfolio.

Johnson, S. R. (2004). *Mind wide open: Your brain and the neuroscience of everyday life*. New York: Scribner.

Jones, W. (2008). *Keeping found things found: The study and practice of personal information management*. Amsterdam: Morgan Kaufmann.

Klingberg, T. (2009). *The overflowing brain: Information overload and the limits of working memory*. Oxford: Oxford University Press.

Lehrer, J. (2009). *How we decide*. Boston: Houghton Mifflin Harcourt.

Lester, J. & Koehler, W. C. (2003). *Fundamentals of information studies: Understanding information and its environment*. New York: Neal-Schuman Publishers.

Linden, D. J. (2007). *The accidental mind: How brain evolution has given us love, memory, dreams, and God.* Cambridge, MA: Belknap Press.

Lively, L. (1996). *Managing information overload.* New York: AMACOM.

Macdonald, S. (2000). *Information for innovation: Managing change from an information perspective.* Oxford: Oxford University Press.

MacDonald, M. (2008). *Your brain: The missing manual: How to get the most of your mind.* Sebastopol, CA: O'Reilly Media.

Marchand, D. A. (Ed.) (2000).*Competing with information: A manager's guide to creating business value with information content.* London: John Wiley & Sons.

Marchand, D. A., Kettinger, W. J., & Rollins, J. D. (2001). *Information orientation: The link to business performance.* Oxford: Oxford University Press.

Marchand, D. A., Kettinger, W. J., & Rollins, J. D. (2001). *Making the invisible visible: How companies win with the right information, people and IT.* London: John Wiley & Sons.

Marcus, G. (2008). *Kluge—The haphazard construction of the human mind.* Boston, MA: Houghton Mifflin Company.

Martin, A. & Rader, H. (Eds.) (2003). *Information and IT literacy: Enabling learning in the 21st century.* London: Facet Publishing.

Mayer-Schönberger, V. (2009). *Delete: The virtue of forgetting in the digital age.* Princeton, NJ: Princeton University Press.

Meadows, J. (2001). *Understanding information.* München: Saur, K. G.

Medina, J. (2008). *Brain rules: 12 principles for surviving and thriving at work, home, and school.* Seattle, WA: Pear Press.

Miller, K. A. (2004). *Surviving information overload: The clear, practical guide to help you stay on top of what you need to know.* Grand Rapids, MI: Zondervan.

Montague, R. (2007). *Your brain is (almost) perfect: How we make decisions.* New York: Dutton Adult.

Nahl, D. & Bilal, D. (Eds.) (2007). *Information and emotion: The emergent affective paradigm in information behavior research and theory.* Medford, NJ: Information Today.

Pijpers, A. G. M. (2006). *Information usage behavior: Theory and practice.* The Hague: Academic Service.

Pijpers, A. G. M. (2007). *Op informatiedieet: Naar een beter gebruik van informatie* (English: *On an information diet: Toward a better use of information*). Amsterdam: Business Contact.

Pijpers, A. G. M. (2009). *Slaap je slim! Hoe win je tijd zonder iets te missen* (English: *Sleep yourself smart! How to win time without missing anything*). Amsterdam: Nieuw Amsterdam.

Pijpers, A. G. M. (2010). *Informatiegedrag van mensen: Hoe mensen informatie zoeken, vinden en delen* (English: *Information behavior of people: How people search, find, and share information*). The Hague: Sdu Publishers.

Pink, D. (2005). *A whole new mind: Why right-brainers will rule the future.* New York: Riverhead.

Pinker, S. (2007). *The stuff of thought: Language as a window into human nature.* New York: Viking Adult.

Pollar, O. (2003). *Surviving information overload: How to find, filter, and focus on what's important (A fifty-minute series book).* Menlo Park, CA: Crisp Publications.

Ratey, J. J. & Hagerman, E. (2008). *Spark: The revolutionary new science of exercise and the brain.* New York: Little, Brown and Company.

Restak, R. (2006). *The naked brain: How the emerging neurosociety is changing how we live, work, and love.* New York: Three Rivers Press.

Restak, R. (2009). *Think smart: A neuroscientist's prescription for improving your brain's performance.* New York: Penguin Books.

Rock, D. (2009). *Your brain at work: Strategies for overcoming distraction, regaining focus, and working smarter all day long.* New York: HarperBusiness.

Rosenberg, D. (2003). Early modern information overload. *Journal of the History of Ideas*, 64(1), 1–9.

Shenk, D. (1998). *Data smog: Surviving the information glut (revised and updated edition).* New York: Harper and Collins.

Small, G. & Vorgan, G. (2008). *iBrain: Surviving the technological alteration of the modern mind.* New York: Collings Living.

Spink, A. & Cole, C. (Eds.) (2006). *New directions in human information behavior.* Dordrecht: Springer.

Spink, A. (2010). *Information behavior: An evolutionary instinct.* Dordrecht: Springer.

Stafford, T. & Webb, M. (2004). *Mind hacks: Tips & tricks for using your brain,* Sebastopol, CA: O'Reilly Media.

Tidline, T. J. (1999). The mythology of information overload. *Library Trend*, 47(3), 485–506.

Weinberger, D. (2007). *Everything is miscellaneous: The power of the new digital disorder.* New York: Times Books.

Wright, A. (2007). *Glut: Mastering information through the ages.* Washington, D.C.: Joseph Henry Press.

Wurman, R. S. (1989). *Information anxiety.* New York: Bantam Doubleday Dell Publishing Group.

Wurman, R. S. (2000). *Information anxiety 2.* Indianapolis, IN: Que.

INDEX